D1430794

Signal Processing of Speech

Signal Processing of Speech

F.J. Owens

BSc, PhD, CEng, MIEE
Senior Lecturer
Department of Electrical and Electronic Engineering
University of Ulster
Jordanstown, Northern Ireland

McGraw-Hill, Inc.

New York   San Francisco   Washington, D.C.   Bogotá
Caracas   Mexico City   San Juan   Toronto

1 2 3 4 5 6 7 8 9 0   DOC/DOC   9 8 7 6 5 4 3

ISBN   0-07-047955-0

First published 1993 by THE MACMILLAN PRESS LTD.
Houndmills, Basingstoke, Hampshire RG21 2XS
and London.

Printed and bound by R. R. Donnelley & Sons Company.

To order or receive additional information on these or any other McGraw-Hill titles, in the United States please call 1-800-822-8158. In other countries, contact your local McGraw-Hill representative.   MH92

To
Mary,
Niall, Gareth, Niamh and Darren

Contents

Preface   xi

1 The Nature of Speech   **1**
  1.1 Introduction   1
  1.2 Mechanism of speech production   3
  1.3 Source–filter model of speech production   5
  1.4 Speech sounds   7
  1.5 Co-articulation and prosody   9
  1.6 Time waveforms and frequency spectra   11
  1.7 The human auditory system   13

2 Digital Speech   **17**
  2.1 Sampling   18
  2.2 Pre-sampling filter   21
  2.3 Quantisation   22
    2.3.1 Uniform quantisation   23
    2.3.2 Logarithmic quantisation   25
  2.4 Adaptive quantisation   28
  2.5 Differential quantisation (DPCM)   29
  2.6 Adaptive differential quantisation (ADPCM)   30
  2.7 Delta modulation   31
  Problems   34

3 Parametric Speech Analysis   **35**
  3.1 Pre-emphasis   36
  3.2 Filter banks for short-time spectral analysis   37
  3.3 Discrete Fourier transform (DFT)   44
  3.4 Fast Fourier transform (FFT)   50
  3.5 Cepstral analysis of speech   53
  3.6 The autocorrelation function   58
  3.7 Linear predictive analysis (LPA)   59
  3.8 Pitch-synchronous analysis   67
  Problems   68

4 Feature Extraction   **70**
   4.1 Short-time energy function   70
   4.2 Zero-crossing rate   71
   4.3 Endpoint detection   72
   4.4 Vector quantisation   72
   4.5 Formant tracking   74
   4.6 Pitch extraction   78
       4.6.1 Gold–Rabiner pitch extractor   79
       4.6.2 Autocorrelation methods   81
       4.6.3 The SIFT algorithm   84
       4.6.4 Post-processing of pitch contours   85
   4.7 Phonetic analysis   85

5 Speech Synthesis   **88**
   5.1 History of speech synthesis   88
   5.2 Formant synthesisers   92
   5.3 Linear predictive synthesisers   100
   5.4 Copy synthesis   101
   5.5 Phoneme synthesis   102
   5.6 Concatenation of multi-phonemic units   107
   5.7 Text-to-speech synthesis   108
   5.8 Articulatory speech synthesis   111
   Problems   120

6 Speech Coding   **122**
   6.1 Sub-band coding   123
   6.2 Transform coding   125
   6.3 Channel Vocoder   127
   6.4 Formant vocoder   129
   6.5 Cepstral vocoder   130
   6.6 Linear predictive vocoders   130
       6.6.1 The LPC-10 algorithm   132
       6.6.2 Multi-pulse and RELP vocoders   134
   6.7 Vector quantiser coders   136

7 Automatic Speech Recognition   **138**
   7.1 Problems in ASR   138
   7.2 Dynamic time-warping (DTW)   140
       7.2.1 Isolated word recognition   141
       7.2.2 Pattern matching   141
       7.2.3 Speaker-independent recognition   146
       7.2.4 Pattern classification (decision rule)   147
       7.2.5 Connected-word recognition   147

7.3 Hidden Markov models   152
    7.3.1 Word recognition using HMMs   155
    7.3.2 Training hidden Markov models   162
7.4 Speaker identification/verification   163
7.5 Future trends   166
    7.5.1 Front-end processing   167
    7.5.2 Hidden Markov models   168
    7.5.3 Neural networks   169
    7.5.4 Speech understanding   171
Problem   172

References   174

Index   176

Preface

The relatively new area of speech processing has undergone significant advances in the three decades that have passed since the advent of digital computing in the early 1960s. The last few years have witnessed the transfer of speech technology from the research laboratory to the marketplace. A variety of commercial speech products is now available for speech synthesis, speech recognition and speech coding. This has been made possible by developments in techniques for speech processing, coupled with the significant advances in microprocessor and digital signal processing (d.s.p.) technology.

The aim of this book is to provide an introduction to the techniques and algorithms used in the design of speech systems. The target readership is students studying speech processing in final year undergraduate and postgraduate degree courses in Electrical and Electronic Engineering, Physics and Computing Science. It is hoped that the book will also be of use to anyone beginning to work or carry out research in speech technology. Readers outside these disciplines may find it suitable for general interest reading.

Speech signal processing depends on certain mathematical, systems and communications principles which have to be understood for a proper appreciation of the area. In writing this book, I have tried to minimise, simplify and illustrate the mathematical content. Speech technology is a multi-disciplinary topic, requiring a knowledge of such diverse areas as signal processing, electronics, computing science, linguistics and physiology. While most of these areas are referred to and briefly described in this book, the emphasis is very firmly on the signal processing aspects of speech technology, reflecting the title and my own personal interests. I regret any imbalance that this may cause, but in a short introductory book, it is impossible to cover everything. When writing, I was constantly aware of having to condense important topics or indeed omit them altogether, because of limited space. I hope that this will not detract too much from the value of the book.

The origin of part of this book is courses of lectures, which I have been giving in final year undergraduate and postgraduate courses in Electrical and Electronic Engineering and Computing Science at the University of Ulster in recent years. During that time, I have received a lot of valuable student feedback which I gratefully acknowledge and which has influenced my treatment of certain topics. I would like to express my gratitude to Bob Linggard who introduced me to the field of speech processing and who has given me valuable support and encouragement. I am indebted to a number of colleagues, postgraduate and undergraduate students, whose research and project work has made a significant contribution to my understanding of speech signal processing; in particular, I would like to thank David Irvine, Sean Murphy, Neville Ramsey, George Wright, Peter Donnelly, Gary Shannon and Kieran Cooney who also generated some of the diagrams. I should like to acknowledge also the authors of numerous research papers and articles, which I have studied and which have provided me with invaluable insight into the challenging area of speech processing. Unfortunately, in an introductory book of this type, I cannot cite all of them individually.

Finally, I would especially like to thank my wife, Mary, for her constant support and encouragement and who, with one finger, typed the entire manuscript from my illegible scrawl.

F.J. Owens

1 The Nature of Speech

He gave man speech and speech created thought
Which is the power of the universe.
P.B. Shelley

1.1 Introduction

Man's amazing ability to communicate through speech sets him apart from other earthly species and is often regarded as a sign of his spirituality. As the most natural form of communication between humans, speech is a subject which has attracted much interest and attention over many years. The structure of speech, its production and perception mechanisms have long occupied linguists, psychologists and physiologists. Scientists and engineers have endeavoured to construct machines which can synthesise and recognise human speech. In recent years, this goal has begun to be realised, though the systems that have been built are still a long way from being able to emulate human performance. Current speech synthesis systems are capable of producing reasonably intelligible though not natural-sounding speech. Automatic speech recognition systems can currently recognise with reasonable accuracy words spoken in isolation from a small vocabulary. Their performance degrades quite significantly, however, when they are required to cope with large vocabularies, continuous speech input and a wide variety of speakers. Nevertheless, the performance of both speech recognition and synthesis systems is improving slowly and steadily with time, and speech systems are now being used in certain commercial applications.

There are three main areas in speech technology – speech synthesis, speech recognition and speech coding. The ultimate goal in speech synthesis is to develop a machine which can accept as input a piece of English text and convert it to natural-sounding speech, which would be as intelligible and as natural-sounding as if spoken by a person. Applications of speech synthesis include speech output from computers, reading machines for the blind and public messaging systems.

The ultimate goal in automatic speech recognition is to produce a system which can recognise, with human accuracy, unrestricted, continuous speech utterances from any speaker of a given language. One of the main

1

application areas for speech recognition is voice input to computers for such tasks as document creation (word processing), database interrogation and financial transaction processing (telephone-banking). Other applications include data entry systems for automated baggage handling, parcel-sorting, quality control, computer aided design and manufacture, and command and control systems.

Speech coding is concerned with the development of techniques which exploit the redundancy in the speech signal, in order to reduce the number of bits required to represent it. This is important when large quantities of speech are to be held on digital storage media, such as voice mail systems, or when a limited bandwidth is available to transmit the signal over a telecommunications channel, such as a cordless telephone channel or a mobile radio channel.

This book describes the main principles and techniques that are used in all three areas of speech technology, and the layout of the book is such that the three areas may be studied more or less independently, though some coding techniques are based on speech synthesis principles.

In chapter 1, the nature of speech, its production and perception are described. Chapter 2 describes methods for converting speech from analogue to digital form and covers speech sampling and various quantisation schemes.

Chapters 3 and 4 describe techniques and algorithms for extracting vocal tract and excitation information from the speech signal and these lie at the heart of systems for speech recognition and coding and to a lesser extent speech synthesis. Chapter 3 is concerned with parametric speech analysis techniques and covers filterbanks, the discrete and fast Fourier transform methods, the autocorrelation function and the important technique of linear prediction. Chapter 4 describes feature extraction methods including pitch and formant frequency estimation and segmentation of the speech into basic sound units.

Chapter 5 is devoted to speech synthesis and covers formant and linear predictive synthesis devices as well as methods for generating control parameters to drive these devices from a phonetic or textual input.

Chapter 6 covers the topic of speech coding and describes a variety of methods for efficiently encoding the speech signal, including subband coding, transform coding, the channel vocoder, the cepstral vocoder and various linear predictive coders.

The final chapter, chapter 7, describes techniques and systems for automatic speech recognition. Much of the chapter is devoted to the two predominant speech processing techniques, dynamic time warping (DTW) and hidden Markov Modelling (HMM), which have become well established for acoustic pattern matching in speech recognition systems. The related topic of speaker identification/verification is also covered in this chapter.

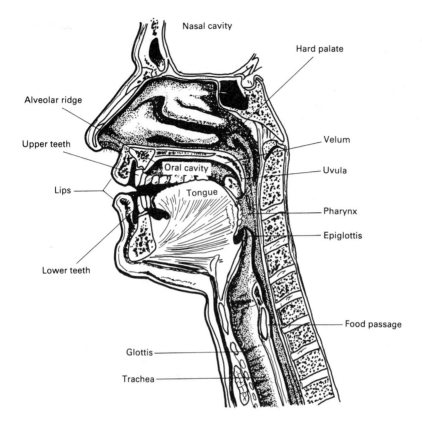

Figure 1.1 Vocal organs

1.2 Mechanism of speech production

A diagram of the vocal apparatus is shown in figure 1.1. It consists essentially of the lungs, trachea (windpipe), the larynx and the oral and nasal tracts. The *larynx* contains two folds of skin called the *vocal cords* which can be made to repeatedly blow apart and flap together as air is forced through the slit between them which is called the *glottis*. The *oral tract* is a non-uniform acoustic tube, approximately 17 cm long in an adult male, terminated at the front by the lips and at the back by the vocal cords or larynx. Its cross-sectional area can be varied from zero to about 20 cm² by muscular control of the speech articulators (lips, tongue, jaw and velum). The *nasal tract* is also a non-uniform acoustic tube of fixed area and length (about 12 cm in an adult male). It is terminated at the front by the nostrils and at the rear by a movable flap of skin called the *velum*, which controls the acoustic coupling between the oral and nasal tracts.

During the production of non-nasalised sounds, the velum seals off the nasal tract and there is a single sound transmission path via the lips. In the production of nasal sounds, the velum is lowered and the nasal tract is acoustically coupled to the oral tract. However, in this situation, the front of the oral tract is completely closed and there is again only a single sound-transmission path via the nostrils. For sounds which are nasalised, sound emanates from both the lips and the nostrils.

In speaking, the lungs are filled with air by muscular expansion of the rib-cage and lowering of the diaphragm. As the rib-cage contracts, air is expelled and is forced along the trachea (windpipe) and through the glottis. This flow of air is the source of energy for speech generation. It can be controlled in different ways to produce various modes of excitation for the vocal system.

Speech sounds can be divided into three broad classes according to the mode of excitation.

(a) **Voiced sounds**, like the sound you make when you say 'aah' or 'oh', are produced when the vocal cords are tensed together and they vibrate in a relaxation mode as the air pressure builds up, forcing the glottis open, and then subsides as the air passes through. This vibration of the cords produces an airflow waveform which is approximately triangular. Being periodic, or at least quasi-periodic, it has a frequency spectrum of rich harmonics at multiples of the fundamental frequency of vibration, or pitch frequency, and decaying at a rate of approximately 12 dB/octave. The vocal tract acts as a resonant cavity which amplifies some of these harmonics and attenuates others to produce voiced sounds. The rate at which the vocal cords vibrate depends on the air pressure in the lungs and the tension in the vocal cords, both of which can be controlled by the speaker to vary the pitch of the sound being produced. The range of pitch for an adult male is from about 50 Hz to about 250 Hz, with an average value of about 120 Hz. For an adult female the upper limit of the range is much higher, perhaps as high as 500 Hz.

(b) In the production of **unvoiced sounds** the vocal cords do not vibrate. There are two basic types of unvoiced sound – fricative sounds and aspirated sounds. For fricative sounds, as for example when you say 's' or 'sh', a point of constriction is created at some point in the vocal tract and, as air is forced past it, turbulence occurs which causes a random noise excitation. Since the points of constriction tend to occur near the front of the mouth, the resonances of the vocal tract have little effect in characterising the fricative sound being produced. In aspirated sounds, as for example that which occurs in the 'h' of 'hello', the turbulent airflow occurs at the glottis as the vocal cords are held slightly apart. In this case, the resonances of the vocal tract modulate the spectrum of the random noise. This effect can be clearly heard in the case of whispered speech.

(c) **Plosive sounds**, as for example the 'puh' sound at the beginning of the word 'pin' or the 'duh' sound at the beginning of 'din', are produced by creating yet another type of excitation. For this class of sound, the vocal tract is closed at some point, the air pressure is allowed to build up and then suddenly released. The rapid release of this pressure provides a transient excitation of the vocal tract. The transient excitation may occur with or without vocal cord vibration to produce voiced (such as d̲in) or unvoiced (such as p̲in) plosive sounds.

1.3 Source–filter model of speech production

A very simple model of the vocal tract, when producing an 'eh' or neutral vowel sound, is a uniform tube or pipe of length L (figure 1.2), with a sound source at one end (the vocal cords) and open at the other (the lips). Such a pipe has odd frequency resonances of f_0, $3f_0$, $5f_0$, . . . etc., where $f_0 = c/4L$, c being the velocity of sound in air. For a typical vocal tract, length $L = 17$ cm and taking $c = 340$ m/s gives resonant frequency values of 500 Hz, 1000 Hz, 1500 Hz, . . . etc. In the vocal tract, these resonances are referred to as *formants*. Of course, the vocal tract can take up many different shapes which give rise to different resonant or formant frequency values and hence different sounds. Thus in continuous speech, the formant frequencies are constantly changing.

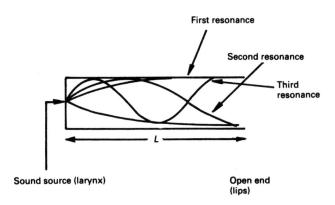

First resonance

Second resonance

Third resonance

L

Sound source (larynx)

Open end (lips)

Figure 1.2   Uniform tube (pipe) model of vocal tract

The preceding discussion leads to the idea of viewing the speech-production process in terms of a *source–filter model* (figure 1.3) in which a signal from a sound source (either periodic pulses or random noise) is filtered by a time-varying filter with resonant properties similar to that of

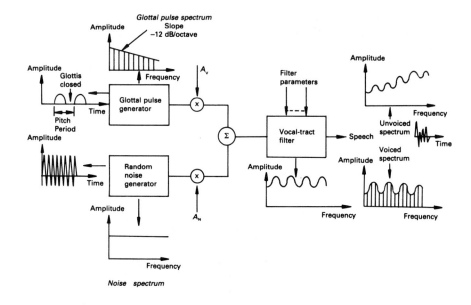

Figure 1.3   Source–filter model of speech production

the vocal tract. Thus the frequency spectrum of the speech signal can be obtained by multiplying the source spectrum by the frequency characteristic of the filter. This is illustrated in figure 1.3 for both voiced and unvoiced speech. The gain controls A_V and A_N determine the intensity of the voiced and unvoiced excitations respectively.

Although the vocal tract has an infinite number of resonances or formants it is only necessary to consider the first three or four, covering the frequency range 100 Hz to about 3.5 kHz, since the amplitudes of the higher formants in the speech signal are almost completely attenuated by the voiced source characteristic which has a high-frequency roll-off of approximately −12 dB/octave. In the case of the unvoiced source, whose spectrum is relatively broad and flat, the same number of formants still suffice although for proper modelling of unvoiced speech it is often necessary to extend the frequency range of interest to about 7 or 8 kHz. An additional point worth making here is that the filter in the source–system model of figure 1.3 models not only the transmission characteristics of the vocal tract but also the effects of radiation from the mouth. The effects of the acoustic radiation impedance may be modelled approximately as a first-order high-pass characteristic, increasing at a rate of 6 dB/octave in the range 0–3 kHz.

The source–filter model is an over-simplification of the speech production process. As already mentioned, the fricative sounds are not filtered by the resonances of the vocal tract to the same extent that voiced and aspirated sounds are, and so the source–filter model is not very accurate for fricative sounds. In addition, the source–filter model assumes that the source is linearly separable from the filter and that there is no interaction between them. This is not strictly true since the vibration of the vocal cords is affected by the sound pressure inside the vocal tract and there is coupling between the vocal tract and the lungs during the period when the glottis is open, thereby modifying the filter characteristics every cycle of the excitation. However, very often these secondary factors are ignored and the source–filter model is perfectly adequate.

1.4 Speech sounds

At a linguistic level, speech can be viewed as a sequence of basic sound units called *phonemes*. It is important to realise, however, that phonemes are abstract linguistic units and may not be directly observed in the speech signal. The same phoneme may give rise to many different sounds or *allophones* at the acoustic level, depending on the phonemes which surround it. Also, different speakers producing the same string of phonemes convey the same information yet sound different as a result of differences in dialect and vocal tract length and shape. Since the shape of the vocal tract, and hence the sound produced, is controlled by the speech articulators, phonemes correspond directly to articulatory positions and movements called *articulatory gestures*. Articulatory gestures may be either static or dynamic events depending on whether or not the articulators move.

Like most languages, English can be described in terms of a set of 40 or so phonemes or articulatory gestures as illustrated in table 1.1 which gives the IPA (International Phonetic Alphabet) symbol for each phoneme together with sample words in which they occur.

The *vowel* gestures are produced by voiced excitation of the vocal tract with the position of the articulators remaining static. There is no nasal coupling and sound radiation is from the mouth. In some languages, French for example, the vowels may or may not be nasalised. The tongue shape remains fairly fixed and each vowel is characterised by the forward/backward and raised/lowered positions of the tongue. Vowels may be classified as front, middle or back depending on the forward–backward positioning of the tongue during articulation. At the acoustic level, each vowel is characterised by the values of the first three or four resonances (formants) of the vocal tract.

The *semivowels* /w, j, r, l/ are also vowel-like gestures. The *glides* /w/ and /j/, like diphthongs, are also dynamic sounds except that the articulators move much more rapidly from one static vowel position to another.

Table 1.1 The phonemes of British English

Vowels		Diphthongs		Fricatives	
Front				Voiceless	
/i/	feet	/ɛi/	say	/s/	sit
/ɪ/	did	/ai/	sigh	/ʃ/	ship
/ɛ/	red	/əʊ/	row	/f/	fat
/æ/	mat	/aʊ/	bough	/θ/	thin
		/iɜ/	deer	/h/	hat
		/uə/	doer		
		/ɔi/	toy		
		/ɛə/	dare		
Middle		Affricates		Voiced	
/ɜ/	heard	/dʒ/	jug	/v/	van
/ʌ/	cut	/tʃ/	chum	/z/	zoo
/ə/	the			/ð/	this
				/ʒ/	azure
Back		Nasals		Plosives Voiced	
/a/	card	/m/	man	/b/	bad
/ð/	cod	/n/	now	/d/	din
/ɔ/	board	/ŋ/	sing	/g/	gone
/ʊ/	wood				
/u/	rude				
Semivowels					
Glides				Unvoiced	
/w/	went			/p/	pin
/r/	ran			/t/	ton
				/k/	kill
Liquids					
/l/	let				
/j/	you				

The *liquids* /r/ and /l/ are essentially static gestures with the oral tract partially closed at some point.

Diphthongs are a combination of two vowel sounds. They are therefore similar to vowels except that the gesture is created when the articulators move slowly from one static vowel position to another.

The *nasals* /m, n/ are produced by vocal-cord excitation with the vocal tract totally constricted at some point along the oral passageway. The velum is lowered so that sound is radiated from the nostrils. Thus the oral cavity acts as a side-branch resonator that traps acoustic energy at certain frequencies. In the sound radiated from the nostrils, these resonant frequencies of the oral cavity appear as anti-resonances or zeros.

When turbulent air-flow occurs at a point of constriction in the vocal tract the class of sounds produced are referred to as *fricatives*. The point of the constriction occurs near the front of the mouth and its exact location characterises the particular fricative sound that is produced. The vocal tract is divided into two cavities by a noise source at the point of constriction. Sound is radiated from the lips via the front cavity. The back cavity traps energy at certain frequencies and so introduces anti-resonances (zeros) into the perceived sound. The unvoiced fricatives /f, θ, s, ʃ/ are produced without vocal-cord vibration whereas in their voiced counterparts /v, ð, z, ʒ/ the vocal cords are vibrating. The phoneme /h/ may be regarded as an unvoiced fricative even though it does not have a voiced counterpart. It is produced with turbulent excitation at the glottis and with the articulatory position of the vowel which succeeds it.

Plosives, or stop-consonants, are generated by forming a complete closure of the vocal tract, allowing the air pressure to build up and then releasing it suddenly. The presence or absence of vocal-cord vibration distinguishes the voiced stops /b, d, g/ from their unvoiced counterparts /p, t, k/. The point of closure in the vocal tract determines the voiced/unvoiced plosive that is produced. Plosives are characterised by transient bursts of energy and as a result their properties are highly influenced by the sounds which precede or succeed them.

The final class of articulatory gestures is the *affricates*. There are two of these in English, the unvoiced affricate /tʃ/ as in the word <u>ch</u>ur<u>ch</u> and the voiced affricate /dʒ/ as in the word <u>j</u>u<u>dg</u>e. These sounds are produced when a stop and fricative consonant are both shortened and combined. In this respect, they may be interpreted as the consonant equivalent of a diphthong.

1.5 Co-articulation and prosody

The description of speech that has been given so far is very much an idealised one. Speech is much more than a simple sequence of articulatory gestures from the set given in table 1.1. As already mentioned, the manifestation of each gesture at the acoustic level is greatly influenced by the surrounding gestures. In normal speech production, the target articulatory positions for many of the gestures will never be actually reached. As a particular gesture is being produced, the next is already being anticipated and this modifies the way in which the articulators move. To a lesser extent, an articulatory gesture may also depend on the preceding one. This phenomenon is known as co-articulation and results in a smearing of sounds into one another. It also gives rise to an effect called allophonic variation, that is, each phoneme may have many different allophones depending on the phonemes which surround it. For example, the 'l' sound in the word 'leap' and the word 'lawn' are the same phoneme, yet are different allophones. (Note how the position of the tongue anticipates the following vowel in each case.)

Co-articulation is mainly responsible for making speech sound natural rather than stilted. As yet, its exact mechanism is not entirely understood and it is proving difficult to simulate adequately in the production of synthetic speech. It is also one of the main reasons why it is proving so difficult to build speech recognisers that can handle continuous speech.

Speech viewed as a sequence of smeared articulatory gestures still does not give the complete picture. Superimposed on the basic sequence of gestures are variations in intonation or pitch (the fundamental frequency of vibration of the vocal cords), rhythm or timing (whether the speech is uttered quickly or slowly) and intensity or loudness. These variations in an utterance are collectively known as *prosody* and can greatly influence its meaning.

Intonation and rhythm can be combined to emphasise certain gestures and produce an effect called *stress*. For example, in the sentence 'I don't have a black pen but I have a blue one', stress would be put on the words 'black' and 'blue'. Rhythm on its own can affect the syntax of a word and helps to distinguish nouns from verbs, such as extract v. extract·, and adjectives from verbs, such as separate v. separate. Intonation can have an effect on meaning too. Pitch very often rises towards the end of a question, the extent and abruptness of the rise depending on whether actual information or confirmation is required in the answer. For example, contrast the utterances 'It's a nice day, isn't it?' and 'This is the right train, isn't it?'. In the first case the pitch does not rise so significantly at the end of the sentence whereas in the second case, where information is required, the pitch rise is much greater and more abrupt.

Very often in normal speech the prosodic pattern is also used to convey the emotional state and attitude of the speaker. Through our 'tone of voice' we can indicate sarcasm, anger, joy, sadness, fear etc., though the exact mechanism is once again not very well understood.

Like co-articulation, the prosodic patterns in speech have a strong influence on its naturalness. In fact without stress and intonation patterns speech sounds monotonous and virtually unintelligible. Rules for assigning prosodic patterns to synthetic speech have been developed but they are still incapable of emulating human naturalness.

1.6 Time waveforms and frequency spectra

Signal processing techniques for speech may be broadly classified as either time-domain or frequency-domain approaches. With a time-domain approach information is extracted by performing measurements directly on the speech signal whereas with a frequency-domain approach the frequency content of the signal is initially computed and then information is extracted from the spectrum. In this section we shall examine briefly the gross features of speech waveforms and speech spectra.

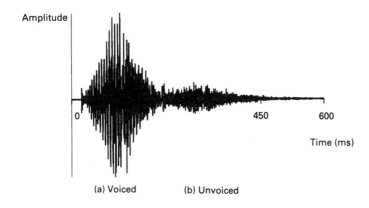

Figure 1.4   Time segments of voiced and unvoiced speech

The time-waveform of a voiced segment of speech from a vowel sound is illustrated in figure 1.4(a). The waveform is clearly periodic with a fundamental frequency equal to that of the pitch frequency. The principal peaks in the waveform correspond to maximum points of excitation of the vocal tract as the vocal cords close rapidly. After each point of maximum excitation, the amplitude of the waveform gradually decays, owing to the damping or losses of the vocal tract. Within each cycle the combined effect of the first three or four vocal-tract resonances (formants) are also observable as ripples or 'ringing' features on the waveform, though they are not readily separable by eye. In contrast to the voiced speech segment, the time-waveform of the unvoiced fricative illustrated in figure 1.4(b) is characterised by a lack of periodicity. Also no resonant structure in the waveform is apparent. It should be pointed out that the features just described are not always so obvious from observing the time-waveform of speech. Very often it is impossible to tell whether the speech is voiced or unvoiced, never mind identifying the points of maximum excitation.

One of the most effective ways of observing the complete frequency spectrum of an utterance is to compute and display its spectrogram. The

Signal Processing of Speech

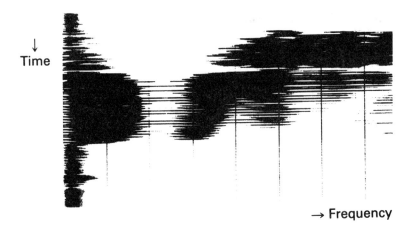

↓
Time

→ Frequency

Figure 1.5   Spectrogram of word 'shed'

spectrogram is in effect a three-dimensional plot illustrating the way in which the frequency spectrum varies with time. The spectrogram of the word 'shed' is given in figure 1.5. The vertical axis represents time and the horizontal axis represents frequency, covering the frequency range 0–5 kHz. The third dimension is given by the darkness of the plot and indicates the energy at a particular time–frequency point. Specifically the darkness of the plot is proportional to the logarithm of the energy and covers a range of approximately 40 dB.

In the vowel sound the formants are observable as dark bands extending horizontally. Movement of the formant frequencies, due to co-articulation, at the transitions between the fricative /ʃ/ and the vowel and between the vowel and the voiced stop /d/ are also observable. The fricative is charac- terised by wideband high-frequency energy with no evidence of formant structure. The voiced stop /d/ appears on the spectrogram as a period of silence corresponding to the closure followed by a burst of high-frequency energy and observable formant structure due to the voicing. The fine vertical bands of energy in the voiced segments are due to the maximum points of excitation during each glottal cycle. Thus the spacing between these bands changes in accordance with the pitch frequency changes. Figure 1.6 shows an alternative way of observing the frequency spectrum of speech. Cross-sections of the original spectrogram at 20 ms time-intervals are taken and plotted on a three-dimensional graph. Valuable information can also be obtained from this type of plot but it is generally less useful than a conventional spectrogram.

A spectrogram is an extremely powerful way of obtaining a visual pattern of an utterance. Two utterances that sound similar have similar

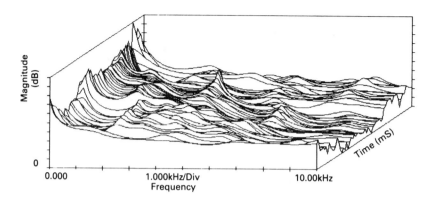

Figure 1.6   Three-dimensional spectrogram of word 'shed'

spectrograms. In fact some phoneticians have learned to read spectrograms with amazing accuracy, that is they are able to work out what was said by studying the spectrogram. However, this process relies heavily on the powerful visual pattern recognition techniques of the human eye and brain. Designing a computer algorithm to emulate this process is a substantially more difficult problem!

1.7 The human auditory system

In the human hearing process, sound pressure waves impinge upon the human ear, where they are converted to a sequence of electrical impulses, which are passed through the nervous system to the brain. Here they are processed and decoded.

The periphery of the human auditory system is illustrated in figure 1.7. The ear is divided into three main regions – the outer ear, the middle ear and the inner ear. The outer ear consists of the *pinna* (the visible part) and the *auditory canal* or *meatus*, which leads to the *eardrum* or *tympanic membrane*. Sound waves travel along the auditory canal and impinge upon the eardrum, causing it to vibrate. The deflection of the eardrum is typically a few nanometres (10^{-9} m) and a low whisper may only cause a maximum deflection equal to one-tenth the diameter of a hydrogen molecule!

In the middle ear, a small bone called the *hammer* (*malleus*) is attached to the eardrum. Upon movement of the eardrum, the hammer makes contact with another bone called the *anvil* (*incus*), causing it to rotate. The anvil in turn is connected to another small bone called the *stirrup* (*stapes*),

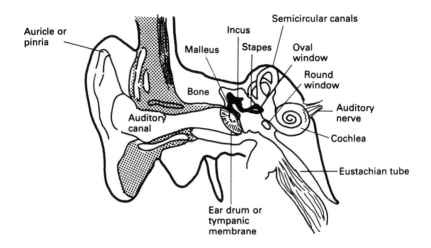

Figure 1.7   The peripheral auditory system

which is attached to the oval window of the inner ear. These three bones (hammer, anvil and stirrup) are the smallest bones in the human body and are called *ossicles*. Their function is to convey the vibrations of the eardrum to the oval window of the inner ear.

The *oval window* is a membrane-covered opening in the bony wall of a spiral-shaped structure called the *cochlea*. The fluid-filled cochlea is divided along its length by two membranes called *Reissner's membrane* and the *basilar membrane*. The vibrations of the oval window cause pressure waves to propagate through the cochlear fluid and these pressure waves cause the basilar membrane to deflect at different points along its length. Attached to the basilar membrane is the *organ of Corti*. This jelly-like organ contains some 30 000 *hair cells* arranged as three rows of outer cells and one row of inner cells. Each hair cell has many tiny hairs protruding from it. The hairs are bent by the motion of the basilar membrane and this creates action potentials in the hair cells. The hair cells are in contact with the *nerve-endings* (*dendrites*) of the neurons of the auditory nerve and the action potentials cause *neural firings* (a series of electrical impulses), which are transmitted via the auditory nerve to the brain.

From the brief description given above, it is clear that the motion of the basilar membrane plays an important role in the hearing process. A good deal of information on its mechanical properties has been determined from psychophysical investigations. It is approximately 35 mm long and is non-uniform along its length, with its base end (nearest oval window) being narrower and more rigid than the apex (inner tip). Thus, the compliance (stiffness) changes gradually along its length, with the result that different points respond differently to different audio frequencies. When a pure audio tone (sinewave) is heard, different points on the membrane vibrate at the frequency of the input tone, with the point of maximum displacement depending on the frequency of the tone. High frequencies produce maximum displacement at the basal end, while low frequencies produce maximum displacement near the apical end. Thus, the basilar membrane performs a form of frequency analysis on a complex input signal, by detecting the different frequency components at different points along its length. Each point can be considered as a bandpass filter with a certain centre frequency and bandwidth. The frequency responses of different points have been measured experimentally and shown to be bandpass responses with approximately constant-Q characteristics. (Q stands for 'quality factor' and refers to the sharpness of the bandpass frequency response; it is the ratio of centre frequency to bandwidth and 'constant' refers to the effect that each filter has the same Q-value.) The responses have been found to be asymmetrical about the centre frequency with the high-frequency roll-off being much steeper than the low-frequency roll-off. The position of the maximum displacement along the membrane varies in a non-linear fashion with frequency. It has been found that the relationship is approximately logarithmic, with linear increments of distance corresponding to logarithmic increments in frequency.

The very low Q-factor of the frequency response curves as measured experimentally would tend to suggest the frequency discriminating properties of the hearing mechanism is very low, which conflicts with our common experience and indeed with properly-conducted psycho-acoustic experiments. It is possible to detect small changes in frequency of a single tone and indeed to hear individual frequency components in a complex tone. This suggests that there must be other auditory processes, which help to sharpen the broad frequency–selectivity curves of the basilar membrane. This is indeed borne out by experiments which attempt to measure quantitatively the ways in which one sound is obscured or rendered inaudible by another. These investigations show that the threshold of hearing for one tone is raised in the presence of another adjacent (masking) tone. The amount by which the threshold must be raised depends on how close the tones are in frequency, and frequencies outside a certain band have negligible effect on the threshold of hearing. In other words, only a narrow band of frequencies surrounding the tone contributes to the masking effect. This band of frequencies is referred to as the *critical band*. Frequency components of a signal falling inside the critical band influence the perception of those in the band, but frequency components falling outside do not. The value of the critical band depends on the frequency of the test tone. For example, at a frequency of 100 Hz, the critical band is approximately 90 Hz, whereas at a frequency of 5 kHz, it is approximately 1000 Hz. The critical bands at a wide range of frequencies have been determined from psycho-acoustic experiments and are plotted in figure 1.8. These critical

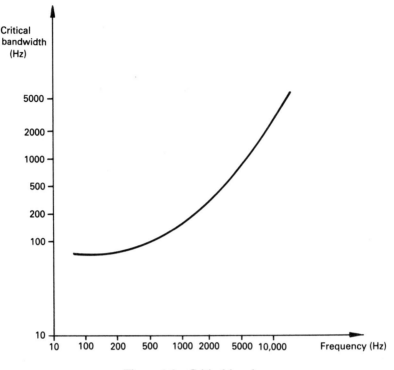

Figure 1.8   Critical bands

band values are much narrower than those suggested by the observed vibration patterns on the basilar membrane.

The exact mechanism or location of the masking process is not yet clearly understood. It is thought that it may be due to a process called *lateral suppression*, in which the neural activity due to weak inputs (basilar membrane deflections) to one group of neurones is suppressed by stronger inputs to adjacent neurones. Whatever the mechanism, it is appropriate to view the processing of the peripheral auditory system in terms of a bank of bandpass filters, whose responses overlap and whose 'effective bandwidths' are given approximately by the critical band values. This is often the basis for designing filterbanks for speech processing.

A suitable source for further reading on the human auditory system is the book edited by J.V. Tobias (1970).

2 Digital Speech

The progressive developments in digital electronics and digital computing since the 1960s have resulted in the conversion from analogue to digital technology of devices for storing and processing audio signals. Many modern tape-recorders and disk-players use digital rather than analogue techniques. Digital transmission of speech is being used to an increasingly large extent on the Public Services Telephone Network (PSTN), and telecommunication systems, in general, are increasingly becoming digital in nature. Most signal processing operations are now carried out using digital computers or special-purpose digital signal processing (DSP) devices.

The most basic requirement in all of the above situations is to convert the analogue speech signal into a digital format in which it is represented by a sequence of numbers. The conversion involves two processes – sampling and quantisation. This two-stage process is sometimes referred to as pulse code modulation (PCM). Sampling is the process of obtaining values of the analogue signal at discrete instants of time, and quantisation refers to the conversion of the amplitude at each sampling instant into a discrete binary number with a specified bit-length. The questions that immediately arise are: how often should the speech signal be sampled and how many bits should be used in the quantisation process? These are the main issues that are addressed in this chapter.

Storing, processing and transmitting signals digitally offers significant advantages. Digital technology is more advanced and more powerful than analogue technology. Digital signals are less sensitive to transmission noise than analogue signals. It is easy to error-protect and encrypt digital signals so that digital transmission can be made very secure. In addition, digital signals of different types can be treated in a unified way and, provided adequate decoding arrangements exist, can be mixed on the same channel. This approach is the main feature of the Integrated Services Digital Network (ISDN) which, at the time of writing, is being developed and implemented. The ISDN can handle, for example, speech, image and computer data on a single channel.

One disadvantage of digital communication is that it requires greater channel bandwidth. This can be several times the bandwidth of an equivalent analogue channel. Thus in digital communications there is a strong emphasis on techniques and systems which compress the channel band-

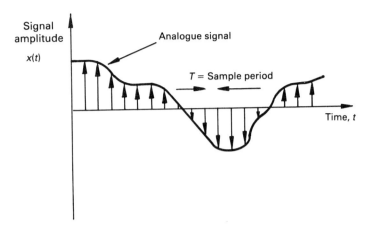

Figure 2.1   Illustration of sampling process in time-domain

width required to transmit the signal. We will return to this topic later in this chapter, and again in much more detail in chapter 6.

2.1 Sampling

The process of sampling a signal is illustrated in figure 2.1. Sampling is carried out at discrete intervals of time T, where T is known as the sample period. The number of samples per second or the sampling frequency f_s in Hz is equal to the reciprocal of the sample period, that is $f_s = 1/T$. The value of the sampling frequency to use in a given situation is determined by Nyquist's sampling theorem, which states that if the highest frequency component present in the signal is f_h Hz, then the sampling frequency must be at least twice this value, that is $f_s \geq 2f_h$, in order that the signal may be properly re-constructed from the digital samples. In other words, the minimum number of samples that is required to represent a sinusoid is 2 samples per cycle as illustrated in figure 2.2(a). If fewer samples are used then a phenomenon known as *aliasing* occurs where a signal of a certain frequency may appear as a lower frequency upon re-construction. This is illustrated in figure 2.2(b). The solid line shows a sinusoid which is sampled at less than the Nyquist rate. If the signal were to be re-constructed from the samples, then the lower-frequency signal indicated by the broken line could result. Therefore the component takes on a different identity and is an alias of the true component. If aliasing occurs in a complex signal such as speech, unwanted frequency components are inserted which distort the signal.

The proof of Nyquist's theorem may be easily shown if we consider the process of sampling as being mathematically equivalent to multiplying the

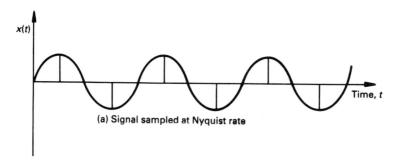

(a) Signal sampled at Nyquist rate

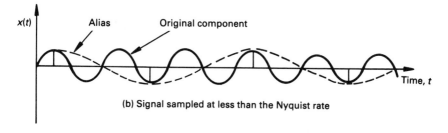

(b) Signal sampled at less than the Nyquist rate

Figure 2.2   Illustration of Nyquist's sampling theorem

signal by a unit impulse train $\sum_{n=-\infty}^{\infty} \delta\,(t - nT)$. Suppose that the original signal has a band-limited spectrum $X(\omega)$, in which the highest radian frequency component is ω_h as shown in figure 2.3(a). For mathematical purposes, it is necessary to consider the double-sided frequency spectrum which has both positive and (theoretical) negative frequencies. The spectrum of the sampled signal may be computed by introducing the unit impulse train and multiplying it by the speech signal, $x(t)$, under the Fourier integral, that is

$$X_s(\omega) = \int_{-\infty}^{\infty} \left\{ \sum_{n=-\infty}^{\infty} \delta\,(t - nT) \right\} \cdot x(t)\,e^{-j\omega t} dt \qquad (2.1a)$$

$$= \sum_{n=-\infty}^{\infty} x(nT)\,e^{-j\omega nT} \qquad (2.1b)$$

Thus the Fourier transform integral becomes a Fourier transform sum, where the time-variable is discrete, but the frequency variable remains continuous. The effect of the sampling on the original spectrum $X(\omega)$ can be obtained by substituting the Fourier series of the impulse train $\left\{ \sum_{m=-\infty}^{\infty} 1/T\,e^{jm\omega_s t} \right\}$ into equation (2.1a). This gives

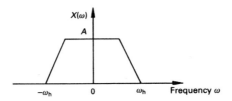

(a) Spectrum of original analogue signal

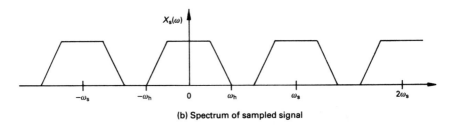

(b) Spectrum of sampled signal

Figure 2.3   Illustration of effect of signal sampling in frequency-domain

$$X_s(\omega) = \int_{-\infty}^{\infty} \left\{ \sum_{m=-\infty}^{\infty} 1/T \, e^{jm\omega_s t} \right\} \cdot x(t) e^{-j\omega t} dt$$

$$= \int_{-\infty}^{\infty} \sum_{m=-\infty}^{\infty} 1/T \, x(t) \, e^{-j(m\omega_s - \omega)t} dt$$

$$= 1/T \sum_{m=-\infty}^{\infty} X(\omega + m\omega_s) \qquad (2.2)$$

where $\omega_s = 2\pi/T$ is the radian sampling frequency. This result indicates that the spectrum of the sampled signal consists of the original base-band spectrum $X(\omega)$ replicated at integer multiples of the sampling frequency, as illustrated in figure 2.3(b). It is clear that the individual replications of the base-band response would overlap if the radian sampling frequency was less than $2\omega_h$. This undesirable situation is shown in figure 2.4, where it can be seen that low-frequency components in the first replication appear as high-frequency components in the base-band signal. This is the aliasing phenomenon referred to earlier. The aim therefore in any sampling situation is to choose the sampling frequency such that the individual replications of the base-band spectrum do not overlap. For this to occur, the sampling frequency ω_s must be greater than twice the highest frequency present in the signal, that is $\omega_s \geq 2\omega_h$.

For many signals, including speech, the highest frequency component is not distinctly known and it is therefore necessary to band-limit the signal

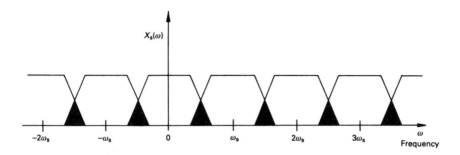

Figure 2.4 Illustration of aliasing

by filtering it prior to digitisation. The analogue filter employed in such a situation is normally called an anti-aliasing or pre-sampling filter. The requirements of this filter for speech processing applications is discussed in the next section.

2.2 Pre-sampling filter

In general, speech contains frequency components with significant energies up to about 10 kHz. However the spectra of the majority of speech sounds only have significant spectral energy content up to about 5 kHz. Furthermore, only the fricative and aspirated sounds exhibit significant spectral energy above this value. Speech band-limited to 5 kHz is perfectly intelligible and suffers no significant degradation. Telephone speech is band-limited to 3.3 kHz and although the transmission of speech through the telephone network degrades its quality significantly, it still remains largely intelligible, since the information-bearing formants are concentrated in the region below 3.3 kHz.

Depending on the application, the sampling rate f_s for speech will normally lie in the range 6–20 kHz. In all such situations, a pre-sampling or anti-aliasing filter is required in order to remove frequency components above the Nyquist frequency, that is $f_s/2$. This analogue filter has the typical amplitude response characteristic shown in figure 2.5. The response in the passband should be reasonably flat, in order to prevent distortion due to certain frequency components being emphasised more than others. The stopband attenuation should be somewhere in the range 60–70 dB, as this is the perceptual dynamic range of speech. Since it is impossible to realise an ideal 'brickwall' filter characteristic, a guardband between the passband and stopband is used. This is usually achieved by choosing the passband edge frequency of the filter to be slightly less than the Nyquist frequency. For speech digitisation, the response of figure 2.5 is most

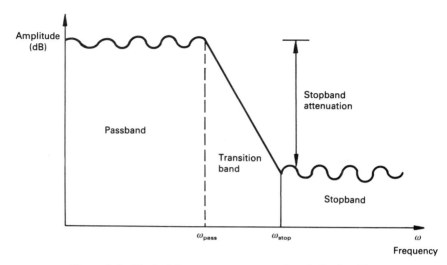

Figure 2.5   Typical frequency response of anti-aliasing filter

economically realised as an elliptic filter of order 6–10, depending on the sampling rate, the guardband used and the stopband attenuation required. An elliptic filter exhibits ripples in both the stopband and passband. The passband ripple should be limited to about 0.5 dB and stopband attenuation, determined by the maximum value of the stopband ripple, should be in excess of 60 dB. Other types of response, such as Butterworth or Chebychev, can also be used, but the complexity of the filters are somewhat greater for an equivalent response realisation. A Butterworth filter has the advantage though of having no passband or stopband ripples and a Chebychev filter has ripples in the passband only.

An alternative to using a highly-specified analogue filter is to use a very simple (low-order) analogue filter, in conjunction with a much higher sampling rate. This is referred to as *over-sampling* and typically values of 5 to 10 times the required sampling rate are used. Conversion of the digital signal to a lower sample rate can be achieved after the signal has been processed by an appropriate digital anti-aliasing filter. Conversion to integer fractions of the sampling rate can be achieved by simply discarding the unwanted samples.

2.3 Quantisation

Quantisation involves converting the amplitude of the sample values into digital form using a finite number of binary digits (bits). The number of bits used affects the speech quality as well as the number of bits per second (bit-rate) required to store or transmit the digital signal. Two types of quantisation will be discussed in this section – uniform quantisation and logarithmic quantisation.

2.3.1 Uniform quantisation

In uniform quantisation, the amplitude range is split into 2^N distinct levels, as shown in figure 2.6, where N is the number of bits used to represent each digitised sample. The output of the quantiser x^q is a binary representation of the nearest quantisation level to the input signal value x. Two's-complement arithmetic is often employed, allowing positive portions of the input signal to be represented by positive digital values and negative portions by negative digital values. In this case, the maximum value of the quantiser output is $2^{(N-1)} - 1$ and the minimum value is $-2^{(N-1)}$. These values correspond to maximum and minimum input signal values of $\{2^{(N-1)} - 1\}/2^{N-1}V_{\text{ref}}$ and $-V_{\text{ref}}$ respectively, where V_{ref} is the d.c. reference voltage applied to the analogue-to-digital converter. The difference between successive quantisation levels, that is $x^q_{i+1} - x^q_i$, is known as the quantiser step-size, δ, and is given by

$$\delta = 2V_{\text{ref}}/2^N \tag{2.3}$$

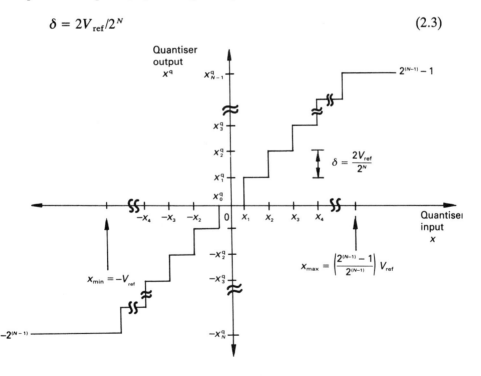

Figure 2.6 Quantisation levels in a uniform quantiser

From figure 2.6, it is clear that all signal values within a given quantiser level will produce exactly the same digital output. In other words, all signal input values between x_i and x_{i+1} will produce the quantised output x_i^q. This gives rise to an associated uncertainty or error for each output. Alternatively, it may be viewed as noise, which is added to the input signal by the quantiser. For an N-bit quantiser, the error for each sample lies in the range $-1/2\{2V_{ref}/2^N\}$ and $+1/2\{2V_{ref}/2^N\}$, as illustrated in figure 2.6. For a sufficiently large number of levels, it may be assumed that the error is uniformly distributed with probability density equal to a constant C over this range. The value of C may be obtained by integrating the probability density function $p(e) = C$ over the complete range and equating the result to unity. Mathematically

$$\int_{-2^{-N}V_{ref}}^{+2^{-N}V_{ref}} p(e)\ \mathrm{d}e\ =\ 1$$

$$\int_{-2^{-N}V_{ref}}^{+2^{-N}V_{ref}} C\ \mathrm{d}e\ =\ 1$$

$$2CV_{ref}\cdot 2^{-N}\ =\ 1$$

$$C\ =\ 2^N/2V_{ref} \qquad (2.4)$$

Having obtained the value of the probability density function, it is now possible to calculate the mean square value of the error, $\overline{e^2}$, by evaluating the integral

$$\overline{e^2}\ =\ \int_{-2^{-N}V_{ref}}^{+2^{-N}V_{ref}} e^2\, p(e)\ \ \mathrm{d}e$$

$$=\ \int_{-2^{-N}V_{ref}}^{+2^{-N}V_{ref}} \{2^N/2V_{ref}\}\, e^2\ \ \mathrm{d}e$$

$$=\ \{2^{-2N}V_{ref}^2\}/3 \qquad (2.5)$$

Suppose the input signal is a sinewave with the maximum allowable peak value of approximately V_{ref}. Such a signal has an r.m.s. value $V_{ref}/\sqrt{2}$ and its mean square value, s^2, is $V_{ref}^2/2$. The signal-to-noise ratio (SNR) is defined as the ratio of the signal power to the noise power and is given by

$$\text{SNR} = \overline{s^2}/\overline{e^2} = \{V_{ref}^2/2\}/[\{2^{-2N}V_{ref}^2\}/3]$$

$$= 1.5 \times 2^{2N} \tag{2.6}$$

Expressing this value in decibels gives

$$\text{SNR}_{dB} = 10\log_{10}\{1.5 \times 2^{2N}\}$$

$$= 10\log_{10}\{1.5\} + 2N\log_{10}2$$

$$= 1.76 + 6.02N \tag{2.7}$$

Thus each additional bit in the quantiser contributes approximately 6 dB improvement in the dynamic range of the analogue-to digital converter. Speech exhibits a dynamic range of some 50–60 dB and therefore in theory 8- or 9-bit quantisation ought to provide the necessary signal-to-noise ratio for good-quality speech. However, referring back to the waveform of a typical speech signal in figure 1.4 it is clear that more bits are necessary because of the peaky nature of the waveform. The mean-square-value of a typical speech signal with peak values approaching that of the maximum allowable value will be much less than a maximum amplitude sinewave. Consequently the signal-to-noise ratio is reduced. In addition, different speakers produce different loudness levels and even the same speaker may produce constantly fluctuating levels. It is thus virtually impossible to use optimally all of the available dynamic range in the analogue-to-digital converter. For these reasons, at least 11- or 12-bit quantisation is generally used in high-quality speech-processing applications.

2.3.2 Logarithmic quantisation

The basic problem with linear quantisation in speech processing is that the quantisation step-size is chosen to accommodate the relatively few peaks in the signal, with the result that low-level signals, such as fricatives, will have a large quantisation error. One solution to this problem is to make the quantiser step-size vary in accordance with the signal amplitude. In other words, the step-size is increased as the signal level increases. Non-uniform quantisation can provide an improved signal-to-noise ratio with a fewer number of bits. This results in a greater efficiency in speech storage and transmission. Ultimately, the speech signal has to be re-converted to its original form and an exact inverse of the quantiser characteristic is required. The process of non-linearly quantising (compressing) a signal and re-constructing (expanding) it is known as companding, which is a contraction of compressing–expanding. Companding devices are now available in single-chip form. These integrated circuits are called 'codecs', which is a contraction of the words <u>co</u>ders–<u>dec</u>oders. They normally use an 8 kHz sampling rate at 8 bits per sample, which corresponds to a bit-rate of 64 kbits/s, and are used widely on digital communications voice links.

There are two widely used companding characteristics – the A-law and the μ-law. The A-law is used largely in Europe and the μ-law in the United States. Both are very similar in nature and performance but unfortunately the world telecommunications authorities cannot agree on a single standard. Both the A-law and the μ-law are based on a logarithmic rather than a linear quantiser characteristic and are described briefly below.

Quantisation using the A-law is based on compressing each input sample $x[n]$ to produce an output sample

$$x'[n] = \frac{A\,x[n]}{1 + \log A}, \qquad 0 \leqslant |x[n]| \leqslant x_{\max}/A \qquad (2.8a)$$

$$= x_{\max} \frac{1 + \log\{A\,|x[n]|/x_{\max}\}}{1 + \log A}\,, \; \text{sgn}\,\{x[n]\}, \frac{x_{\max}}{A} < x \leqslant x_{\max} \qquad (2.8b)$$

where

A is a constant that determines the level of compression ($A = 87.56$ in the European standard),

$x_{\max}$ is the maximum absolute value of the signal,

$|x[n]|$ is the magnitude of $x[n]$,

sgn $\{x[n]\} = \pm 1$, when $x[n]$ is positive or negative respectively.

The corresponding decoder equations can be obtained by inverting equations (2.8) to determine $x[n]$ in terms of $x'[n]$. The μ-law companding equations are different from those of the A-law, though the resulting characteristic is very similar. The μ-law is described by the equation

$$x'[n] = x_{\max} \frac{\log\,\{1 + \mu(|x[n]|/x_{\max})\}}{\log\,\{1 + \mu\}}\, \text{sgn}\,\{x[n]\} \qquad (2.9)$$

where μ is a parameter which determines the level of compression and all of the other symbols have the same meaning as before. A value of $\mu = 255$ is often used.

In a practical system, the companding equations are not used directly on each input sample. Instead, the quantisation intervals are defined using a piecewise linear approximation to the companding equations, as illustrated in figure 2.7 for the A-law for the case of positive sample values. The complete characteristic exhibits odd symmetry about the vertical axis. The positive portion of the characteristic consists of 8 linear segments. The

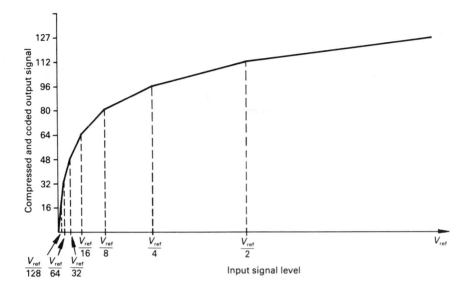

Figure 2.7 Companding curve for *A*-law compander

output signal is represented by an 8-bit code with a maximum positive value of $01111111_2 = 127_{10}$ and a minimum negative value of $10000000_2 = -128_{10}$. For the first segment, relative input signal values from 0 to 1/128 are linearly converted to output values from 0_{10} to 15_{10}. This is exactly equivalent to 12-bit linear resolution. In segment 2, input values from 1/128 to 1/64 are converted to output values from 16_{10} to 31_{10}, which is also equivalent to 12-bit resolution. Similarly segments 3, 4, 5, 6, 7 and 8 correspond to resolutions of 11, 10, 9, 8, 7 and 6 bits respectively. Thus as the input signal level increases; the precision decreases gradually from 12-bits to 6-bits.

Log-PCM codecs are widely used on digital telephony channels. A sampling-rate of 8 kHz is employed and, with 8 bits allocated to each sample, the corresponding transmission or storage rate is 8 kHz × 8 = 64 kbits/s. In order to estimate the bandwidth required to transmit this signal, consider its transmission along an analogue channel. First, it is necessary to convert the digital signal to analogue form and this is carried out using some form of modulation process. A variety of modulation techniques exist and the required bandwidth per bit/s depends on the efficiency of the modulation process. In two-level phase-shift keying (PSK), for example, where one bit (0 or 1) is represented by two different values of the phase of the carrier signal, each bit/s corresponds to 1 Hz of bandwidth. Thus, for a two-level PSK modulation, the required transmission bandwidth for a 64 kbits/s signal is 64 kHz, which is of the order of 16 times the bandwidth required to transmit the 4 kHz bandwidth of the analogue signal. This figure can be reduced by improving the efficiency of the modulation process. For example, a 16-level PSK system, which can be used to represent four bits, reduces the bandwidth by a factor of 4 over the 2-level system, that is the required bandwidth for the 64 kbits/s is reduced to 16 kHz. However, this is still 4 times that of the original signal and is therefore a strong motivation for having techniques which encode the digital signal more efficiently, thereby reducing the bit-rate and preserving bandwidth. Various techniques for bandwidth compression of speech are discussed in some detail in chapter 6 on Speech Coding.

2.4 Adaptive quantisation

The main limitation of the uniform and non-uniform quantisers described in the previous two sections is that they cannot take account of any amplitude variations in the speech signal between different speakers, or even between voiced and unvoiced segments of a signal from the same speaker. A solution to this problem is to adjust (adapt) dynamically the step-size of the quantiser to suit the changing signal characteristics. Alternatively, the input signal can be normalised to effectively reduce its dynamic range before it is quantised. This technique is commonly referred to as adaptive pulse code modulation (APCM). There are two basic adaptation strategies. The adaptation can be performed at every sample or every few samples. This is referred to as *instantaneous adaptation*. Alternatively, since speech can be stationary over relatively long time intervals, the adaption can be carried out every 10–20 ms or so. This is referred to as *syllabic adaptation*.

A block diagram of a basic APCM system is shown in figure 2.8. The input sample $x[n]$ is quantised and coded to $c[n]$ which is processed by step-size adaptation logic to create a signal $q[n]$ that is used to control the step-size of the quantiser. Adaptation of the step-size is carried out by

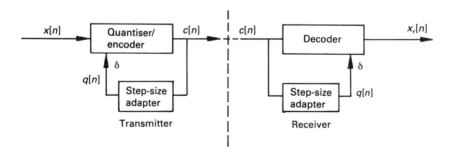

Figure 2.8   Adaptive PCM system (APCM)

multiplying the previous step-size by a constant which is determined by the magnitude of the previous coded sample $c[n-1]$, that is

$$\delta(n) = K \cdot \delta(n-1) \tag{2.10}$$

where K is dependent on $|c[n-1]|$. For small $|c[n-1]|$, a value of $K < 1$ is used to obtain a smaller step-size and hence finer resolution. For large $|c[n-1]|$, a value of $K > 1$ is used to obtain a larger step-size and hence coarser resolution. Depending on the number of bits in the quantiser, many values of K may be defined for different regions of the quantiser. In the decoder, the coded signal $c[n]$ is processed by an inverse quantiser to produce the re-constructed signal $x_r[n]$. The step-size is controlled by the step-size adaptation signal $q[n]$.

As a general rule, APCM gives a reduction of 1 bit per sample over log-PCM for a given signal-to-noise ratio in telephone-quality speech. Alternatively, for a given bit-rate, an improvement of approximately 6 dB in signal-to-noise ratio can be obtained.

2.5 Differential quantisation (DPCM)

An analysis of speech signals shows that there is considerable correlation (similarity) between adjacent speech samples, particularly in regions of voiced speech. Consequently, the difference signal formed by subtracting adjacent samples has a lower variance and dynamic range than the speech signal itself and, for a given signal-to-noise ratio, can therefore be encoded using fewer bits. This feature is exploited in differential PCM (DPCM) by estimating (predicting) the current speech sample, $x[n]$ (instead of using the actual previous sample), subtracting it from the actual current sample $x[n]$ and quantising the difference signal, $d[n]$, as shown in figure 2.9. The re-constructed signal $x_r[n]$ is obtained by adding the quantised difference signal $d[n]$ to the signal estimate $x_e[n]$. x_r is input to the predictor which estimates the next signal sample $x_e[n]$ from its time-history. $x_e[n]$ is normally estimated as a linear combination of the past few samples of x_r, that is

$$x_e[n] = \sum_{k=1}^{N} a_k x_r[n-k] \tag{2.11}$$

A value of $N = 4$ is typical, though as few as one or as many as 14 previous samples may be used in obtaining the signal estimate. In the simplest system $(N = 1)$, the signal estimate is simply a constant times the previous value of the re-constructed signal, that is $x_e[n] = a_1 x_r[n-1]$. The values of the predictor coefficients are heuristically chosen to yield reasonable sample estimates. It is clear that the better the predictor, the more accurate

Signal Processing of Speech

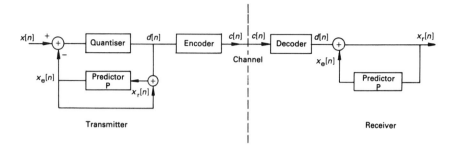

Figure 2.9 Differential PCM system (DPCM)

the value of the signal estimate, the smaller the quantisation error in the difference signal and the better the signal-to-noise ratio will be. Using DPCM, it is possible to obtain an improvement of about 5–6 dB in signal-to-noise ratio or a saving of about 1 bit per sample for a given signal-to-noise ratio. The saving is not as large as might be expected since, in practice, the dynamic range of the error signal can approach that of the signal itself.

2.6 Adaptive differential quantisation (ADPCM)

The DPCM technique described in the previous section uses both a fixed quantiser and a fixed predictor. A substantial improvement can be obtained by adding an adaptive quantiser and/or an adaptive predictor. The resulting systems are all generally referred to as adaptive differential PCM (ADPCM) systems. The block diagram of an ADPCM system incorporating an adaptive quantiser and an adaptive predictor is shown in figure 2.10. Synchronisation of the transmitter and receiver is achieved by having essentially a replica of the receiver embedded in the transmitter and using only the transmitted difference signal in determining step-size adaptation, in both the quantiser and the inverse quantiser, and in predicting the next signal estimate. Step-size adaptation might be typically a mixture of both instantaneous and syllabic adaptation and is achieved by making the adaptation signal $q(n)$ dependent on the magnitude of the difference signal as well as its rate of change. In this way, the system can adapt better to both stationary and non-stationary speech. The predictor coefficients may be calculated and updated every 10–20 ms, by solving a set of linear equations (see section 3.8). Alternatively, they may be updated every sample, using an optimisation algorithm, which uses a hill-climbing (gradient) technique to minimise the error between the signal estimate and the actual signal.

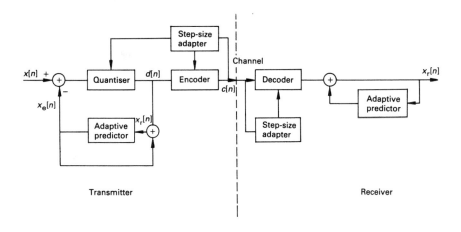

Figure 2.10   General ADPCM system

The complexity of an ADPCM system is directly related to the complexity of the predictor algorithm. Low-to-medium complexity systems use an adaptive quantiser and a fixed predictor and are capable of reproducing speech with slightly less than telephone-quality at 3/4 bits/sample at an 8 kHz sampling rate (24 kbits/32 kbits/s). High-complexity systems, using an adaptive quantiser and an adaptive predictor and operating at 32 kbits/s, can improve the signal-to-noise ratio further and can reproduce speech with better than telephone-quality. The telecommunications standards organisation, CCITT (International Telegraph and Telephone Committee) has established an ADPCM standard for voice and data transmission at 32 kbits/s over the telephone network. The standard accepts log-PCM speech at 64 kbits/s and converts it to 32 kbits/s, using an ADPCM technique. Currently, it is possible to implement the complete algorithm on a single digital signal processing integrated circuit.

2.7 Delta modulation

Delta modulation (DM) is a special or limiting case of the differential PCM (DPCM) technique described in section 2.5. In a DM system, the predictor in figure 2.9 is a first-order predictor, so that

$$x_e[n] = a x_r[n-1] \qquad (2.12)$$

where a is a constant with a value slightly less than 1 and the quantiser is a 1-bit quantiser or hard-limiter, which outputs a step-size of $+\delta$ (1) if the

Signal Processing of Speech

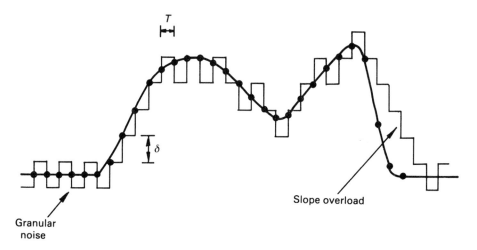

Figure 2.11   Illustration of delta modulation

difference signal is positive and a step-size of $-\delta$ (0) if it is negative as illustrated in figure 2.11. Since a 1-bit quantiser is used, the bit-rate of a DM system is simply equal to the sampling rate, but the sampling rate must be several times that of a conventional PCM system. If the sampling rate is too low, a condition known as *slope overload* may occur, where the system is incapable of tracking a fast-changing signal. The overload can be reduced by using either a higher sampling rate or a larger step-size. However, the use of a larger step-size increases the 'granular noise', due to the alternate 1s and 0s, which is particularly noticeable when no input is present.

At low signal-to-noise ratios, the bit-rate for delta modulation is slightly lower than that of log-PCM. However, for signal-to-noise ratios approaching or greater than telephone-quality, the required bit-rate is higher. The scope of application for DM systems is therefore severely limited. Its main advantage is that it is very simple and economical to implement.

An improvement in delta modulation can be obtained by adapting the step-size of the quantiser in a manner similar to that discussed in section 2.4. One strategy might be to double or halve the step-size depending on whether the next 1-bit quantiser output will be different from or equal to the last output, that is

$$\delta[n] = 2\ \delta[n-1], \qquad c[n] \neq c[n-1] \tag{2.13}$$
$$= 1/2\ \delta[n-1], \qquad c[n] = c[n-1]$$

where the step-size $\delta[n]$ is normally constrained to have a value between certain pre-determined maximum and minimum values, that is $\delta_{min} \leqslant \delta[n] \leqslant \delta_{max}$. In a rapidly changing signal condition, the step-size can increase quickly up to its maximum value, δ_{max}, reducing the possibility of overload. During silence, the step-size is decreased to its minimum value, δ_{min}, which determines the level of granular noise in the idle condition. Adaptive DM (ADM) systems using very simple algorithms are capable of reproducing speech of very good quality at bit-rates in the range 32 kbits/s to 48 kbits/s.

The main drawback with adaptive delta modulation is that since the step-size can vary instantaneously with sudden changes in the input signal, the system can take a long time to recover from transmission errors, which causes degradation of the speech quality. A solution to this problem is to make the step-size variation slower than the instantaneous variation in the speech signal. This has the effect of increasing the likelihood of slope-overload distortion, but leads to a reduction in the level of granular noise. The step-size control signal is effectively generated by low-pass filtering the step-size changes indicated, by observing the most recent (3–5) bit outputs of the quantiser. The time-constant of the low-pass filter is typically of the order of 5–10 ms. Systems employing these principles are generally known as continuously variable slope delta modulation (CVSD) systems. The basic adaption algorithm of CVSD systems can be written as

$$\delta[n] = \beta \, \delta[n-1] + a[n] \, \delta_0 \qquad (2.14)$$

where δ_0 is a constant. β is another constant with a value very close to 1; a value of $\beta = 0.99$ corresponds to low-pass filtering with a filter time-constant of 10 ms. $a[n] = 1$ or 0, depending on whether a certain number of similar bits were observed in the most recent bits. The algorithm for deriving the value of $a(n)$ is generally known as the JKL algorithm, in which $a[n]$ is held at 1 for L samples, irrespective of its calculated value for the next $L-1$ samples, if at least K similar bits occurred in the previous J bits. Thus during slope overload adaptation of the step-size is relatively rapid and increases to a maximum value

$$\delta_{max} = \delta_0 / \{1-\beta\} \qquad (2.15)$$

When $a[n] = 0$, the step-size decreases at a rate determined by β, until a specified minimum step-size δ_{min} is reached, at which point the system becomes a conventional DM system, until the input causes the step-size to increase again.

CVSD systems can produce log-PCM quality speech at about 40 kbits/s and slightly less than telephone-quality at 32 kbits/s. This does not represent any improvement over ADM. However, CVSD can prove useful for communications-quality speech at bit-rates of 16 kbits and below. Added attractions of CVSD in this area of application are its simplicity and its robustness to transmission errors when used on a noisy channel.

Problems

2.1. (a) A sinusoidal signal of frequency 1 kHz is sampled at a frequency $f_s = 10$ kHz beginning at time $t = 0$. Determine the first ten values of the sampled sequence.
(b) Show that a sinusoid of frequency 11 kHz sampled in the same way as in (a) is an alias of the 1 kHz sampled signal.

2.2. A complex signal whose highest significant frequency is known to be 450 Hz is to be sampled and processed digitally. Calculate suitable sampling rates if the anti-aliasing filter used is of order

(i) 8   and   (ii) 1

In the case of (ii), how might the sample rate of the digital signal be reduced to that of (i)?

2.3. In a particular high-quality digital speech processing system, a signal bandwidth of 7 kHz and a signal amplitude resolution of 0.05 per cent covering the voltage range ±5 V are required. Uniform quantisation is to be used. Determine:
(a) the minimum sampling rate;
(b) the minimum number of bits per sample;
(c) the quantiser step-size;
(d) the r.m.s. value of the quantisation noise;
(e) the dynamic range of the A/D converter in dB.

2.4. Suppose that, owing to the peaky nature of the waveform and general amplitude fluctuations, the speech signal occupies on average only 30 per cent of the dynamic range of the A/D converter in problem 2.3. If the signal-to-noise ratio is to be no worse than before, calculate the required number of bits per sample.

3 Parametric Speech Analysis

All the application areas of speech technology, including speech recognition, speech synthesis and speech coding, require some form of preliminary analysis of the speech signal. This chapter describes the basic techniques that are normally used to extract acoustic information directly from the speech signal. Most of these techniques are based on the source–filter model of speech production which was introduced in chapter 1. In this model, the excitation source is assumed to be linearly separable from the transmission characteristics of the vocal tract, which are represented by a quasi-time-invariant filter. The speech waveform itself is then assumed to be the output of this filter in response to the excitation source, which is either a quasi-periodic pulse generator (voiced sounds), a random-noise generator (unvoiced sounds) or, in some cases, a mixture of both (voiced fricatives). 'Speech analysis' is mainly the process of estimating the relatively slowly time-varying parameters which specify the filter, from a speech signal that is assumed to be the output of that filter. Other goals might include voiced/unvoiced classification and pitch-period estimation for voiced speech.

Speech analysis techniques may be broadly classified as either frequency-domain or time-domain approaches. The major goal in speech analysis is to estimate the frequency response of the vocal tract. The techniques of processing the speech signal using a bank of bandpass filters, discrete Fourier transformation (DFT) and homomorphic or cepstral processing can all be used to achieve this. Time-domain measures such as the autocorrelation function, zero-crossing rate and signal energy can also be used to extract limited but useful information about the speech signal. The very important and powerful technique of linear prediction will also be introduced in this chapter. Linear prediction is essentially an efficient time-domain waveform coding technique, but it can be extended to produce an estimate of the frequency spectrum of the signal.

The concept of 'short-time analysis' is fundamental to most speech analysis techniques. The assumption made is that, over a long interval of time, the speech waveform is non-stationary but that, over a sufficiently short time interval (10–30 ms), it can be considered stationary. This is due to the fact that the rate at which the speech spectrum changes is directly related to the rate of movement of the speech articulators (lips, tongue, jaw etc.) and this is limited by physiological constraints. Thus most speech analysis systems operate on a time-varying basis, using short segments of speech selected at uniformly spaced time intervals or frames of typical duration 10–30 ms.

3.1 Pre-emphasis

The description of the source–filter model of speech production in chapter 1 indicates that in the spectrum of voiced speech there is an overall –6 dB/octave trend, as frequency increases. This is a combination of a –12 dB/octave trend due to the voiced excitation source and +6 dB/octave trend due to radiation from the mouth. This means that, for each doubling in frequency, the signal amplitude, and hence the measured vocal tract response, is reduced by a factor of 16. It is therefore desirable to compensate for the –6 dB/octave roll-off by pre-processing the speech signal to give a + 6 dB/octave lift in the appropriate range so that the measured spectrum has a similar dynamic range across the entire frequency band. This is referred to as pre-emphasis. In a digital signal processing system, pre-emphasis can either be implemented as a first-order, high-pass analogue filter with a 3 dB cut-off frequency somewhere between 100 Hz and 1 kHz (the exact position is not critical) which precedes the anti-aliasing filter and A/D converter, or as a digital high-pass filter which processes the digitised speech signal. The high-pass filtering action may be achieved digitally using the difference equation

$$y[n] = x[n] - ax[n-1] \tag{3.1}$$

where $y[n]$ denotes the current output sample of the pre-emphasis filter, $x[n]$ is the current input sample, $x[n-1]$ is the previous input sample and a is a constant usually chosen between 0.9 and 1. Again, the actual value is not too critical. Taking z-transforms of equation (3.1) gives:

$$Y(z) = X(z) - az^{-1}X(z) = (1-az^{-1})X(z) \tag{3.2}$$

where z^{-1} denotes the unit sample delay operator. The transfer function $H(z)$ of the filter is therefore

$$H(z) = Y(z)/X(z) = 1 - az^{-1} \tag{3.3}$$

and its block diagram is given in figure 3.1. An expression for its frequency response may be obtained by putting $z = e^{j\omega T}$, where T is the sample period of the digital speech signal:

$$H(e^{j\omega T}) = 1 - ae^{-j\omega T} \tag{3.4}$$

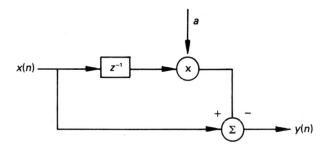

Figure 3.1   Digital pre-emphasis filter

The magnitude of this function is

$$|H(e^{j\omega T})| = |1 - e^{-j\omega T}|$$
$$= [1 + a^2 - 2a \cos \omega T]^{1/2} \tag{3.5}$$

A plot of this frequency response in decibels (dB) with $a = 0.9$ and $T = 100$ μs, for different values of frequency f ($\omega = 2\pi f$) up to half the Nyquist rate, is shown in figure 3.2.

In the case of unvoiced speech, there is no need to apply pre-emphasis, since there is no spectral trend to be removed. However, for simplicity, pre-emphasis is normally applied to unvoiced speech as well.

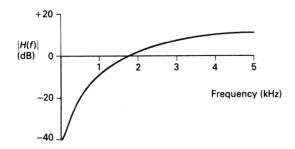

Figure 3.2   Frequency response of digital pre-emphasis filter

3.2 Filter banks for short-time spectral analysis

Figure 3.3 shows the normal method of connecting a bank of bandpass filters to implement a short-time spectrum analyser, where the filter pass-bands are chosen to cover the typical speech frequency band of 0–5 kHz. As few as 4 and as many as 100 or more filters have been used, depending

Signal Processing of Speech

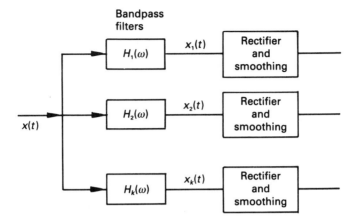

Figure 3.3   A bank of bandpass filters

on the application and the degree of accuracy of hardware complexity required. Very often the spacing and bandwidth of the analysing filters progressively increase with frequency in order to try and mimic the decreasing spectral resolution and definition of the human ear. Table 3.1 gives the specification of a 19-channel filter bank due to Holmes which has been used successfully in a channel vocoder for low bit-rate coding of speech [Holmes, 1980] and as the front-end in an automatic speech recognition system [Bridle *et al.*, 1983].

If the analyser in figure 3.3 were to be an ideal one, then its filters would have rectangular bandpass characteristics with the same constant gain and linear phase in their passbands, and zero gain outside. Hence, the sum of their individual frequency responses (composite response) would be flat with linear phase. In this situation, the input $x(t)$ could be synthesised exactly by adding the bandpass filter outputs $x_k(t)$. However, the realisation of an ideal bandpass filter is impossible, because the slope of its roll-off skirts must be infinite, and it must therefore be of infinite order. In a realisable filter bank, the filters must overlap each other, especially when lower filter orders are to be used.

Before the advent of the digital computer and VLSI integrated circuits for digital signal processing, filter banks for speech analysis were generally implemented using low-order analogue (continuous-time) bandpass filters, the magnitudes of the various spectral components being coarsely measured by rectifying the filter outputs and then low-pass filtering (smoothing) the rectified signals. This approach has been widely used in forming the short-time spectrum for use in various automatic speech recognition (ASR) systems. Figure 3.4 shows the circuit of a single filter-bank channel, consisting of a second-order bandpass filter, a precision rectifier

Table 3.1 Specification of a 19-channel filter bank, after Holmes (1980)

Channel number	Centre frequency	Analysing bandwidth
1	240	120
2	360	120
3	480	120
4	600	120
5	720	120
6	840	150
7	1000	150
8	1150	150
9	1300	150
10	1450	150
11	1600	150
12	1800	200
13	2000	200
14	2200	200
15	2400	200
16	2700	200
17	3000	300
18	3300	300
19	3750	500

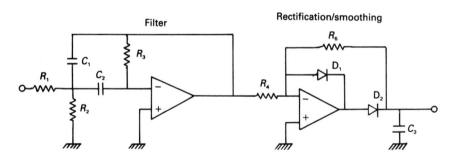

Figure 3.4 Single analogue filter bank channel

and smoothing circuit. The time-varying spectrum of the input speech signal is then estimated by sampling the output of each channel, typically every 10–20 ms. The corresponding time-constant of the smoothing filters is in the range 20–40 ms.

Developments in VLSI integrated circuits have made digital realisations of filter banks more and more attractive. These attractions include: flexibility of design of the individual bandpass filters; precision of realisation; and the stability of digital hardware.

There are a number of methods for designing digital filters – see, for example, Lynn and Fuerst (1989) or almost any text on digital signal processing. One popular method which will be outlined here is the bilinear transformation. In this method the digital filter is designed from an analogue prototype using a transformation which converts the s-domain transfer function of an analogue filter into the z-domain transfer function of an equivalent digital filter using the mapping

$$s = \frac{2 (1 - z^{-1})}{T (1 + z^{-1})} \tag{3.6}$$

where T is the sample rate of the digital filter. The transformation is invertible with

$$z = \frac{1 + (T/2)s}{1 - (T/2)s} \tag{3.7}$$

Putting $s = \sigma + j\omega$ in the above equation gives

$$z = \frac{[1 + (T/2)\sigma] + j\omega T/2}{[1 - (T/2)\sigma] - j\omega T/2} \tag{3.8}$$

For $\sigma < 0$, the modulus of z, $|z|$, is less than 1 so that the left half of the s-plane maps to the inside of a circle of radius 1 (unit-circle). For $\sigma > 0$, $|z|$ is greater than unity and the right half of the s-plane maps to the outside of the unit-circle. With $\sigma = 0$ ($s = j\omega$), $|z| = 1$ and the $j\omega$-axis in the s-plane maps onto the unit-circle in the z-plane. There is a non-linear relationship between the analogue frequency variable ω_a and the digital frequency variable ω_d. Specifically, from equation (3.6) with $s = j\omega_a$ and $z = e^{j\omega_d T}$:

$$j\omega_a = \frac{2(1 - e^{-j\omega_d T})}{T(1 + e^{-j\omega_d T})} = \frac{2j}{T} \tan (\omega_d T/2) \tag{3.9}$$

Therefore

$$\omega_a = \frac{2}{T} \tan(\omega_d T/2) \quad \text{and} \quad \omega_d = \frac{2}{T} \tan^{-1}(\omega_a T/2) \tag{3.10}$$

For small ω, $\tan(\omega_d T/2) \sim \omega_d T/2$ which means that $\omega_a \sim \omega_d$ and the mapping is approximately linear. However, for other than small values of ω, the mapping is non-linear and a warping action occurs. In order to compensate for this, the specification of the digital filter is normally 'pre-warped' when deriving the transfer function of the prototype analogue filter. For example, suppose we wish to design a low-pass digital filter with cut-off frequency ω_{dc}. To compensate for the warping action, the cut-off frequency, ω_{ac} of the prototype analogue is pre-warped to a value $\omega_{ac} = 2/T \tan(\omega_{dc}T/2)$ so that when designed using the bilinear transformation the corresponding digital filter will have the desired cut-off frequency.

The second-order analogue filter in figure 3.4 has an s-domain transfer function

$$H(s) = \frac{bs}{s^2 + bs + \omega_0^2} \tag{3.11}$$

where ω_0 and b are the centre frequency and bandwidth of the filter respectively, both expressed in radians/s. Applying the bilinear transformation to this transfer function (see problem 3.3) yields a digital filter with transfer function

$$H(z) = \frac{Y(z)}{X(z)} = \frac{(a_0 - a_1 z^{-2})}{(1 + b_1 z^{-1} + b_2 z^{-2})} \tag{3.12}$$

where $X(z)$ and $Y(z)$ are the z-transforms of the filter input and output signals respectively. a_0, a_1, b_1 and b_2 are numerical coefficients whose values are given by the expressions

$$a_0 = a_1 = \frac{2bT}{2 + 2bT + \omega_0^2 T^2}$$

$$b_1 = \frac{2\omega_0^2 T^2 - 4}{2 + 2bT + \omega_0^2 T^2} \quad \text{and} \quad b_2 = \frac{1 + \omega_0^2 T^2 - 2bT}{2 + 2bT + \omega_0^2 T^2} \tag{3.13}$$

From equation (3.12) we can write

$$Y[z] \cdot (1 + b_1 z^{-1} + b_2 z^{-2}) = X[z] \cdot (a_0 - a_1 z^{-2}) \tag{3.14}$$

Taking inverse z-transforms and rearranging gives the time-domain filter difference equation

$$y[n] = a_0 x[n] - a_1 x[n-2] - b_1 y[n-1] - b_2 y[n-2] \tag{3.15}$$

which computes the filter output sequence $y[n]$ from the input signal sequence $x[n]$. Note that the computation of the output signal at sample instant n requires not only the value of the input signal at time n but also its value at time $n-2$ and also the values of the filter output at times $n-1$ and $n-2$. The block diagram of this filter is shown in figure 3.5. Its response to a single sample of unity value (unit sample response) consists of an infinite

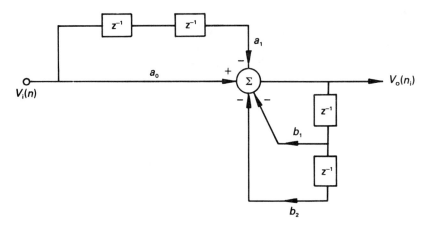

Figure 3.5   Second-order digital bandpass filter

sequence of non-zero output samples and for this reason it is known as an infinite impulse response (IIR) filter.

The use of the bilinear transformation in designing a typical bandpass filter for speech analysis will now be illustrated. Suppose we wished to design a digital filter to implement channel number 7 in the 19-channel filter bank outlined in table 3.1. This is a bandpass filter with a centre frequency of 1000 Hz and a bandwidth of 150 Hz and suppose it is to be second-order and therefore has the s-domain transfer function of equation (3.11). The speech sample rate is 10 kHz ($T = 10^{-4}$s). The required centre frequency ω_{od} and bandwidth b_d of the digital filter are therefore

$$\omega_{od} = 2\pi\cdot 1000 = 2000\pi \text{ rad/s} \quad \text{and} \quad b_d = 2\pi\cdot 150 = 300\pi \text{ rad/s}$$

In order to compensate for the non-linear nature of the bilinear mapping it is necessary to pre-warp these frequencies in the prototype analogue filter. The radian centre frequency ω_{oa} and bandwidth b_a of the prototype analogue filter are both computed using equation (3.10):

$$\omega_{oa} = \frac{2}{10^{-4}} \cdot \tan\{2000\pi\cdot 10^{-4}/2\} = 6498.4 \text{ rad/s}$$

$$b_a = \frac{2}{10^{-4}} \cdot \tan\{300\pi\cdot 10^{-4}/2\} = 943.2 \text{ rad/s}$$

Now using the expressions in equation (3.13), the filter coefficients may be computed:

$$2 + 2bT + \omega_0^2 T^2 = 2 + (2\times943.2\times10^{-4}) + (6498.4\times10^{-4})^2$$

$$= \underline{2.610926026}$$

$$a_0 = a_1 = \frac{2\times943.2\times10^{-4}}{2.610926026} = \underline{0.072247929}$$

$$b_1 = \frac{2(6498.4\times10^{-4})^2 - 4}{2.610926026} = \underline{-1.208542838}$$

$$b_2 = \frac{1 + (6498.4\times10^{-4})^2 - 2\times943.2\times10^{-4}}{2.610926026} = \underline{0.472498268}$$

It is also possible to implement a filter bank using finite impulse response (FIR) filters. These filters have a unit sample response which consists of a finite number of samples only. This is due to the fact that in an FIR filter, the output at any sample instant depends only on the current and previous values of the input and not on previous values of the output. A typical FIR filter structure is shown in figure 3.6. The z-domain transfer function of this filter is

$$H(z) = \sum_{k=0}^{N-1} a_k z^{-k} \tag{3.16}$$

and its difference equation is

$$y[n] = \sum_{k=0}^{N-1} a_k x[n-k] \tag{3.17}$$

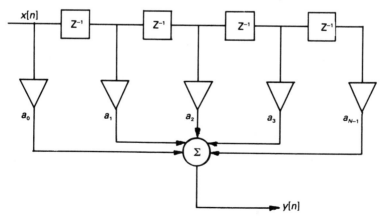

Figure 3.6   Direct form for finite impulse response filters

Various design techniques exist for computing the values of the filter coefficients a_k to meet a particular design specification. FIR filters are generally computationally less efficient than equivalent IIR filters, since a large number of coefficients, N, are required to obtain a sharp roll-off in the filter characteristic. A particular attraction, however, is that they can be designed to have an exactly linear-phase characteristic which means that there will be no phase distortion of the signal by the filter.

It is clear that an IIR digital filter produces a filtered output value for every sample of the signal input. In the case of speech, which may remain fairly stationary over time intervals of the order of 10–20 ms (100–200 samples at a 10 kHz rate), it is unnecessary to compute the spectrum at every sample instant. Therefore, the output samples of each filter in a bank of IIR bandpass digital filters are normally squared and averaged over a period of about 10–20 ms. This is equivalent to rectification, smoothing and re-sampling in an analogue filter bank.

In an FIR filter, the filtered output need not be computed for each sample input as the filter is non-recursive which means that computation of the filter output depends only on the current and previous input sample values and not on previous output sample values. Provided that the filter data are clocked through the delay elements of the FIR filter at the input signal sample rate, computation of the output can take place at any desired rate, for example every 10–20 ms. Filter output averaging is therefore not required in an FIR filter bank.

Because of their computational efficiency and the number of filters involved, IIR filters tend to be favoured in filter banks for speech analysis.

3.3 Discrete Fourier transform (DFT)

The discrete Fourier transform (DFT), normally computed via the fast Fourier transform (FFT) algorithm, is another widely used technique for evaluating the frequency spectrum of speech. In order to understand the operation of the DFT, consider, as a starting point, the standard Fourier transform which gives the frequency spectrum of a continuous time-domain signal. Mathematically, the Fourier transform and its inverse are expressed as

$$X(\omega) = \int_{-\infty}^{+\infty} x(t)e^{-j\omega t}dt; \qquad x(t) = \frac{1}{2\pi} \int_{-\infty}^{+\infty} X(\omega)e^{+j\omega t}dt \qquad (3.18)$$

For the transform to exist, the integral of $x(t)e^{-j\omega t}dt$ must be finite. In many signal processing applications, including speech, it is impossible to satisfy this condition for existence of the transform and it is impractical to specify the signal for all time. Furthermore, if the integration is over infinite time, the time-varying, short-time spectral information will simply be averaged out. All of these problems can be overcome if the signal is truncated and a stationary portion of it is used in the spectral computation. Suppose that this portion of signal consists of N samples of a discrete-time signal with sample period T. The process of sampling can be represented by multiplying the signal by a unit-impulse train and so the transform of the truncated signal may be written as

$$X(\omega) = \int_{-\infty}^{+\infty} \left\{ \sum_{n=0}^{N-1} \delta(t-nT) \cdot x(t) \right\} e^{-j\omega t} dt \qquad (3.19)$$

Since the signal is sampled, its frequency spectrum is periodic and repeats at integer multiples of the sampling frequency $\omega_s = 2\pi/T$. For computation purposes, assume that the spectrum is to be evaluated at N frequencies, linearly spaced between d.c. and the sampling frequency ω_s. If the frequency between successive frequency components is $\delta\omega$ then $N\delta\omega = \omega_s$ and $\omega = k\delta\omega$, $k = 0, 1, 2, \ldots, N-1$:

$$X(k\delta\omega) = \int_{-\infty}^{+\infty} \left\{ \sum_{n=0}^{N-1} x[nT] \cdot \delta(t-nT) \right\} e^{-jk\delta\omega t} dt \qquad (3.20)$$

Interchanging the order of integration and summation gives

$$X(k\delta\omega) = \sum_{n=0}^{N-1} x[nT] \int_{-\infty}^{+\infty} \delta(t-nT) e^{-jk\delta\omega t} dt$$

$$= \sum_{n=0}^{N-1} x[nT] \cdot e^{-jk\delta\omega t} \qquad (3.21)$$

Since $\delta\omega = \omega_s/N$ and $f_s = \omega_s/2\pi = 1/T$, the above equation may be written more simply as

$$X(k\delta\omega) = \sum_{n=0}^{N-1} x[nT] \cdot e^{-j2\pi nk/N}, \qquad k = 0, 1, \ldots, N-1 \qquad (3.22)$$

which is the discrete Fourier transform of the truncated signal. An expression for the inverse discrete Fourier transform (IDFT) may be similarly derived, that is

$$x[nT] = 1/N \sum_{k=0}^{N-1} X(k\delta\omega) \cdot e^{+j2\pi nk/N}, \qquad n = 0, 1, \ldots, N-1 \qquad (3.23)$$

Computing the DFT for an N-point sequence produces a series of complex terms, containing the amplitude and phase information for each spectral component. For real $x[nT]$, this spectral sequence exhibits complex conjugate symmetry about the point $[(N/2)+1]$ and thus there are $[(N/2)+1]$ independent spectral points. Spectral components are spaced $2\pi/NT$

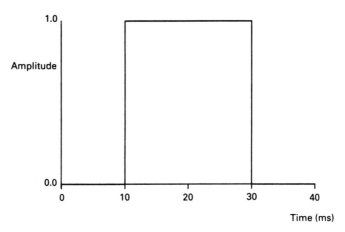

Figure 3.7   Rectangular window function

radians/second apart and the highest component is at π/T radians/second $(\omega_s/2)$.

In computing the DFT of a segment of speech signal of duration NT seconds in the above way, there is an implied 'windowing' of the signal in that only that portion of it seen through the rectangular window of figure 3.7 is used in the transformation. This is equivalent to multiplying, or weighting, the signal by the rectangular function which has a frequency response $H(\omega)$ given by

$$H(\omega) = NT \cdot \frac{\sin(\omega NT/2)}{(\omega NT/2)} \qquad (3.24)$$

The general shape of this response $H(\omega)$ is illustrated in figure 3.8. In frequency-domain terms, the act of time-domain multiplication corresponds to convolving the window response with the signal spectrum. The magnitude of the kth spectral component $|X(k)|$ is a measure of the average strength of this frequency which is present in the signal over the window duration. The spectral components $X(k)$, for k equal to 0 through $N - 1$, then correspond to the set of outputs from an N-channel filter bank, each filter of which has a frequency response similar in form to figure 3.8, with its centre frequency at $\omega_K = 2\pi k/NT$. The side-lobes in the filter characteristic are clearly undesirable since they cause the spectral measurement at any particular analysing frequency to be corrupted by contributions from adjacent frequency components. This is known as 'spectral leakage'. The first side-lobes of the filter characteristic are only about 14 dB down on the main lobe peak and thus the rectangular window is rarely used in practice. Instead a 'soft-windowing' technique, which smoothly tapers the ends of the speech segment to zero, is often employed. There

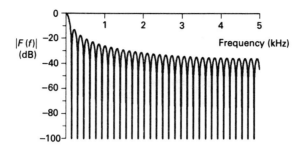

Figure 3.8   Frequency response of rectangular window

are many 'soft-windows' [see, for example, Harris (1978)] which can be used, but a very common one is the Hamming window defined as

$$W[nT] = \{0.54 - 0.46 \cos(2\pi n/N)\}, \quad 0 \leqslant n \leqslant N \qquad (3.25)$$

$$= \qquad 0 \qquad , \quad \text{otherwise}$$

where n is the sample number. The general form of this function is illustrated in figure 3.9 and its frequency response in figure 3.10. The attraction of this particular window stems from the fact that 99.96 per cent of the spectral energy is in the main-lobe and its side-lobes remain more than 40 dB down at all frequencies. However, for a given window duration, the Hamming window gives rise to a filter characteristic whose main lobe is twice that of a rectangular window. It thus trades off main-lobe width for reduced side-lobe ripple.

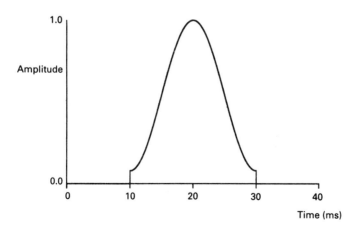

Figure 3.9   Hamming window function

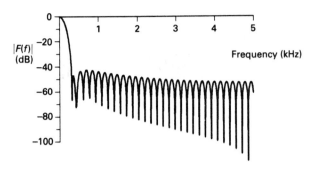

Figure 3.10   Frequency response of Hamming window

From the above it is clear that, having adopted a suitable window shape, the only method of changing the effective filter width is to modify the duration of the window, frequency resolution being inversely proportional to window length. This is illustrated in figure 3.11. Figure 3.11(a) shows a windowed segment of voiced speech. A Hamming window, with $N = 512$

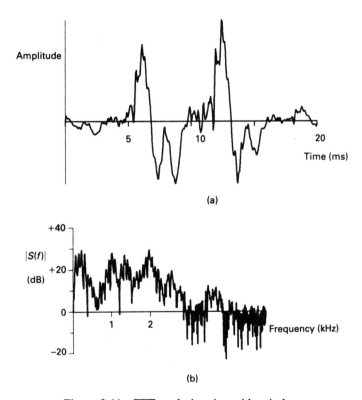

(a)

(b)

Figure 3.11   FFT analysis using wide window

samples at a 10 kHz sampling rate was used. Figure 3.11(b) shows the short-time transform of this segment of speech. The individual harmonics of the pitch-period are resolved as well as the slowly varying characteristic of the vocal tract transfer function. Figures 3.12(a) and 3.12(b) show the windowed speech and the short-time transform for the first 70 samples of the same segment of speech. These samples were multiplied by a Hamming window ($N = 50$) and then augmented with zero values, so that the DFT-size was exactly the same as before. In this case, the frequency resolution is much less. Only the general shape of the vocal tract transfer function is preserved. These examples illustrate the time-domain/frequency-domain trade-off which is always a consideration in the analysis of non-stationary or quasi-stationary signals using the DFT. A long window gives good frequency-domain resolution but poor time-domain resolution, and a short window gives good time-domain resolution but poor frequency-domain resolution. In speech analysis, a window of duration 20

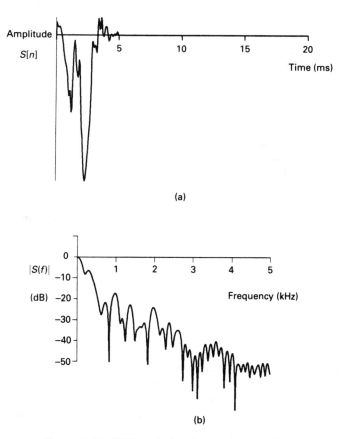

Figure 3.12   FFT analysis using narrow window

ms is generally a good compromise though it is too long to capture information on transient sounds like plosives and stops.

So far only the computation of one spectral section has been considered. To obtain a complete short-time spectral analysis, computation of successive sections is required. One approach is simply to 'slide' the window along the speech waveform and compute an N-point DFT at each time sample. This method is rarely used in a speech processing application because of the excessive amount of computation involved. In any case, we have already seen that speech remains roughly invariant over time intervals of the order of 10–30 ms.

Another approach is to 'hop' the window rather than 'slide' it. Some examples of hopping are illustrated in figure 3.13. Here three possible ways of hopping the DFT computation are illustrated – that is in jumps of the duration of the window, half the duration of the window, or one-quarter the duration of the window. The actual method chosen in practice would depend on the time-domain/frequency-domain compromise referred to earlier and the amount of permissible computation. A common strategy in speech analysis is to use a window of duration 20–30 ms and overlap each window by 10–20 ms.

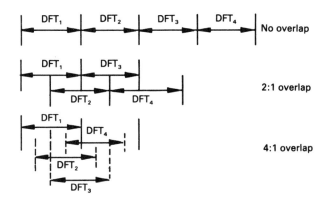

Figure 3.13   Examples of hopping DFTs

3.4 Fast Fourier transform (FFT)

Computing the DFT of N samples of signal involves N^2 calculations, each requiring a complex multiplication and addition. There is therefore a considerable amount of computation involved, especially for large N. Fortunately, a much more efficient algorithm exists for computing the DFT. This is called the fast Fourier transform (FFT) and was developed by Cooley and Tukey (1965). It exploits the inherent redundancy in the DFT and reduces the number of calculations to $N \log_2 N$ which is substantially less than N^2, especially for large N. There is no degree of approximation with the FFT; it provides exactly the same result as the direct calculation. The only restriction is that for maximum efficiency N must be a power of 2, that is $N = 2^m$, where m is an integer.

In order to illustrate the basic principle of the FFT algorithm, consider the basic DFT of an N-point sequence expressed as the sum of two separate DFTs, of length $N/2$, of the even and odd samples. If $E(k)$ denotes the DFT of the even samples and $O(k)$ that of the odd samples, then it may be shown that

$$X(k) = E(k) + W_N^K \cdot O(k) \tag{3.26a}$$

and

$$X(k + N/2) = E(k) - W_N^K \cdot O(k) \tag{3.26b}$$

where $W_N^K = e^{-j2\pi nk/N}$. The quantity W_N^K is often referred to as a 'twiddle factor'. The calculations in equation (3.26) are illustrated in figure 3.14(a). Because of its shape, this is often referred to as an 'FFT butterfly'.

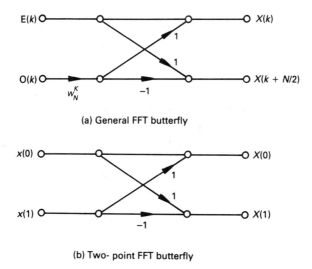

(a) General FFT butterfly

(b) Two- point FFT butterfly

Figure 3.14   FFT butterflies

Calculation of the even and odd transforms requires $N^2/4$ complex operations each and adding them together using the above relationships requires N operations. Thus the total is $(N^2/2) + N$ operations which is considerably less than N^2. However, the saving in computation does not

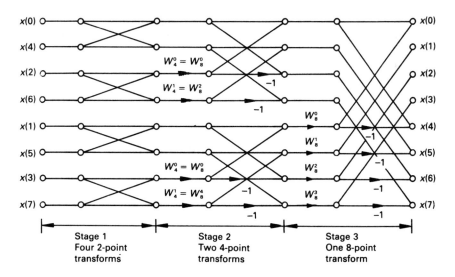

Figure 3.15   Computation of 8-point FFT

end there. The even sequence can itself be broken down into a further even and odd sequence, and likewise the odd sequence. Provided that N is a power of 2, this process can be repeated until the even and odd sequences are of length 2. The computation of the basic two-point DFTs is relatively trivial since the twiddle factors W_N^K of a 2-point DFT are equal to $+1$ and -1 and thus no multiplications are required. Figure 3.14(b) shows the DFT butterfly for a single, 2-point transform. The complete FFT is calculated by computing the requisite number of 4-point transforms from the 2-point transforms and then computing 8-point transforms from the 4-point transforms and so on until the complete N-point transform has been calculated. This process is illustrated diagrammatically in figure 3.15 for the case of an 8-point FFT. Although this is perhaps a rather trivial example, it serves to illustrate many of the principles involved. The sequence of time samples $\{x[0], x[1], x[2], x[3], x[4], x[5], x[6], x[7]\}$ is repeatedly split or decimated into even and odd sequences until four 2-point sequences result. After the first decimation, the even sequence is $\{x[0], x[2], x[4], x[6]\}$ and the odd sequence is $\{x[1], x[3], x[5], x[7]\}$. Then these even and odd sequences are themselves split into even and odd sequences, giving $\{x[0], x[4]\}$, $\{x[2], x[6]\}$, $\{x[1], x[5]\}$ and $\{x[3], x[7]\}$. The DFT of each of these 2-point sequences can now be easily computed using the butterfly in figure 3.14(b). This is stage 1 in figure 3.15. Stage 2 involves computing two 4-point transforms from adjacent pairs of 2-point transforms using the butterfly in figure 3.14(a) (equation (3.26)). The twiddle factors are $W_4^0 (= W_8^0)$ and W_4^1 $(= W_8^2)$. In stage 3, the desired 8-point transform is computed from the two 4-point transforms. The twiddle factors are W_8^0, W_8^1, W_8^2 and W_8^3.

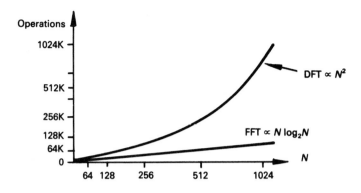

Figure 3.16   Illustration of DFT v. FFT computation

The required number of operations for an N-point FFT is $N\log_2 N$ which is substantially less than N^2, especially for large N. Figure 3.16 illustrates how much faster the FFT is compared with the DFT by plotting N^2 and $N \log_2 N$ as a function of the sequence length N. As already stated, the FFT algorithm is most efficient when the number of time samples N to be transformed is a power of 2. If N is not a power of 2, then it may be padded out with zero samples to the nearest power of 2 before transformation. The action of adding zero samples has no effect on the calculated spectral information; it simply increases the number of points at which the spectrum is evaluated.

The FFT has become a popular technique for spectral analysis because of its computational efficiency. Virtually all commercial software packages for signal processing include modules which are based on the FFT. Also many spectrum analysers use the FFT to compute the frequency spectrum of a signal in real-time at very high sampling rates.

3.5 Cepstral analysis of speech

In considering the DFT in section 3.3 it was intimated that the duration of the analysing window has to span a few pitch-periods of the speech signal in order to obtain good frequency resolution. For voiced speech, this results in a frequency spectrum in which the discrete line spectrum of the periodic excitation is multiplied by the vocal tract spectral envelope (see figure 3.11). In order to extract the vocal tract spectral envelope, a technique for removing the pitch ripple is required. This can be achieved by a technique known as cepstral truncation which will now be described and illustrated.

Let $X(\omega)$ denote the spectrum of the voiced speech signal, $P(\omega)$ the spectrum of the pitch impulses and $H(\omega)$ the spectrum of the vocal tract which includes the effects of glottal waveform shape and radiation from the mouth. The relationship between the magnitude of these three spectra can be expressed simply as follows:

$$|X(\omega)| = |P(\omega)| \times |H(\omega)| \qquad (3.27)$$

Taking the logarithm of this equation gives

$$\log \{|X(\omega)|\} = \log\{|P(\omega)|\} + \log\{|H(\omega)|\} \qquad (3.28)$$

Thus, in the logarithm of $|X(\omega)|$ the contributions due to $|P(\omega)|$ and $|H(\omega)|$ are added. Furthermore, the contribution from $|H(\omega)|$, which is essentially determined by the properties of the vocal tract itself, tends to vary slowly with frequency, while the contribution from $|P(\omega)|$ (pitch) tends to vary more rapidly and periodically with frequency. This leads to the notion that these two components should now be separable by means of a linear filtering operation. This filtering is normally carried out by inverse Fourier-transforming $\log \{|X(\omega)|\}$ to produce what is known as the cepstrum of the signal. The horizontal axis of the cepstrum has the dimensions of time and is termed the quefrency of the signal. In the cepstrum, the contribution due to pitch occurs at multiples of the pitch period, while the contribution due to the vocal tract tends to occur near the origin because it varies much more slowly than the harmonic ripple. If now only the values near the origin in the cepstrum are retained and these values are Fourier-transformed, then the log-spectrum of the vocal tract $(\log\{|H(\omega)|\})$ is obtained.

The block diagram of a cepstral processing system for speech analysis is shown in figure 3.17. Figure 3.18 shows the windowed time-waveform, log-magnitude spectrum, cepstrum and cepstrally-smoothed spectrum for a vowel sound, of 20 ms duration (200 samples at a sampling rate of 10 kHz). Calculating the DFT of the windowed speech segment and taking logar-

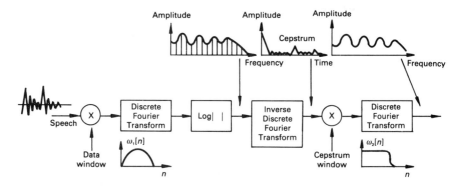

Figure 3.17   Homomorphic system for speech analysis

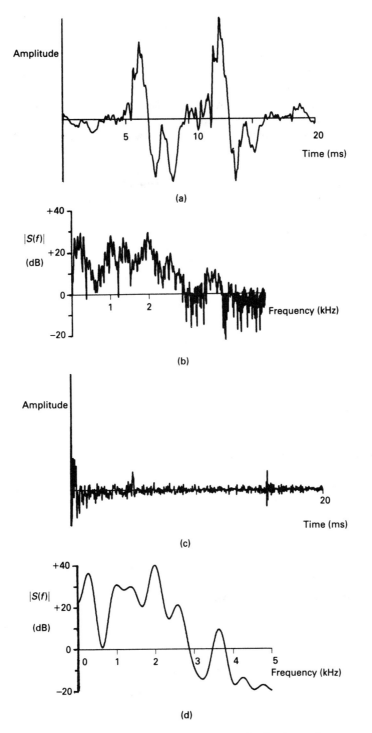

Figure 3.18 Homomorphic filtering of voiced speech

ithms produces the log-magnitude spectrum of figure 3.18(b), in which the slowly-varying component, due to the vocal tract transmission, and the rapidly-varying periodic component, due to pitch, are apparent. As previously discussed, the slowly-varying part of the log-magnitude spectrum, when inverse-transformed, produces the low-time part of the cepstrum (near the origin) – figure 3.18(c) – and the rapidly-varying periodic component manifests itself as a strong peak at a time equal to the period of the input speech segment. For example, from figure 3.18(c) it is clear that the pitch-period of the input speech is approximately 5 ms. In order to produce the cepstrally-smoothed spectrum (vocal tract spectral envelope), the low-time values only of the cepstrum are retained by multiplying the cepstrum by a suitable window. One such window, flat-topped and with a cosine roll-off, is described by the equation

$$W_c[nT] = \begin{cases} 1.0 & , \quad 0 \leqslant nT < T_1 \\ \{1 + \cos(\pi(nT-T_1)/T_2)\}, & T_1 \leqslant nT < (T_1 + T_2) \end{cases} \quad (3.29)$$

where $(T_1 + T_2)$ should be less than the pitch-period in the segment. For the spectra in figure 3.18, values of $T_1 = 2$ ms and $T_2 = 1.5$ ms were used. The truncated sequence is then Fourier-transformed to produce the vocal tract spectral envelope of figure 3.18(d). It is worth mentioning at this point that a very similar result can be obtained by direct smoothing of figure 3.18(b). This process is described in a little more detail in section 4.5.

The results of the same set of operations carried out on a segment of unvoiced speech are shown in figure 3.19. This situation is much the same, with the exception that the random excitation of the input speech produces a rapidly-varying random component in the log-magnitude spectrum – figure 3.19(b). Thus in the cepstrum – figure 3.19(c) – the low-time components correspond as before to the slowly-varying vocal tract transfer function. However, since in this case the rapid variations in the log-magnitude spectrum are not periodic, there is no strong peak as for the voiced speech segment. So the presence or absence of this cepstral peak can give an indication as to whether the speech segment under analysis is voiced or unvoiced. Cepstral analysis can be carried out on a time-varying basis by hopping the analysis-window, usually with overlap, in exactly the same way as for the DFT method described previously.

It is clear that cepstral truncation is an extremely useful method for removing 'pitch ripple' from high-resolution spectra, to leave only the vocal tract transfer function information. However, it trades off temporal resolution for increased spectral resolution, in that the time-window employed must contain at least 2 pitch-periods to produce the original high-resolution spectra. Indeed, if pitch-period is to be estimated from the

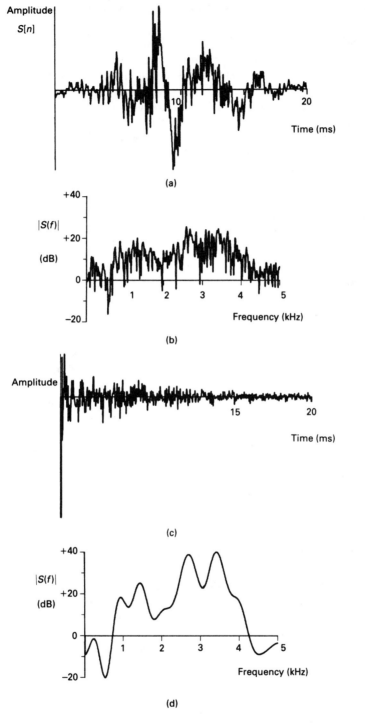

Figure 3.19 Homomorphic filtering of unvoiced speech

cepstrum, then the analysis-window should span at least 4 or possibly more pitch-periods, in order to produce a strong peak in the cepstrum. Consequently, if both pitch-period and spectral-envelope information are to be computed using this method, then two analysing windows are normally employed. The result of using an analysis-window, which spans a few pitch-periods, is that spectral properties and pitch-period are, in a sense, 'averaged' over this time. However, this averaging effect is small and insignificant for the spectral properties and pitch-period changes encountered in normal speech.

3.6 The autocorrelation function

The autocorrelation function (ACF) gives a measure of the correlation of a signal with a delayed copy of itself. The autocorrelation value, $R(k)$, of a stationary signal $x[n]$ for a time-shift of k samples is defined as

$$R(k) = \sum_{n=-\infty}^{\infty} x[n] \cdot x[n + k] \tag{3.30}$$

For the above summation to be computable the signal amplitude must be known for all time, and for the summation to remain finite the signal must have finite energy. As far as speech is concerned, the signal is quasi-stationary, has infinite energy and is not known for all time. In this case, it is appropriate to calculate a short-time autocorrelation function by isolating successive segments (frames) of the signal by multiplying it with a rectangular window, $W(n)$, of width N samples which has a value of 1 in the interval $(0, N - 1)$ and is 0 outside. For a window starting at the beginning of frame m the short-time autocorrelation function is defined as

$$R_m(k) = \sum_{n=0}^{N-1} \{x[n] \cdot W[n]\} \cdot \{x[n + k] \cdot W[n + k]\} \tag{3.31}$$

Figure 3.20 shows plots of this function for both voiced and unvoiced speech. In the case of voiced speech, the short-time autocorrelation function exhibits peaks at time-shifts corresponding to multiples of the pitch-period. At these points the speech signal is in phase with the delayed version of itself, giving high correlation values. It would therefore seem that the short-time autocorrelation function ought to be a powerful technique for estimating the pitch-period of voiced speech. However, there are occasions when it is no easier to detect automatically the peaks in the short-time autocorrelation function than in the time waveform. Despite this, the short-time autocorrelation function forms the basis of some pitch detection algorithms. A number of these will be discussed in the next chapter.

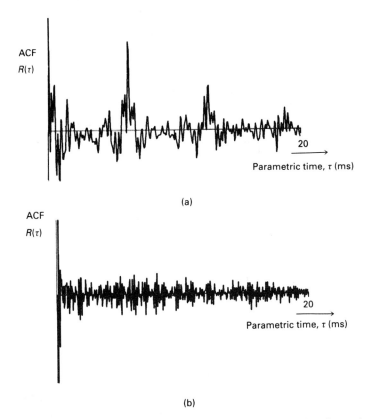

20

Parametric time, τ (ms)

(a)

ACF
$R(\tau)$

20

Parametric time, τ (ms)

(b)

Figure 3.20   Short-time autocorrelation functions for voiced and unvoiced
speech

3.7 Linear predictive analysis (LPA)

In the early 1970s, the technique of linear prediction was shown to be applicable to speech by Atal and Hanauer (1971). It is a very important and powerful speech processing technique which is used in systems for speech synthesis, speech recognition and speech coding. The basic idea behind the method is that sample values of speech, $x[n]$, can be approximated as a linear combination of the past p speech samples as shown in figure 3.21 (a value of $p = 12$ is normally sufficient for both voiced and unvoiced speech). Mathematically, the linear predictor is described by the equation

$$\widetilde{x}[n] = a_1 x[n-1] + a_2 x[n-2] + \ldots + a_p x[n-p]$$

$$= \sum_{k=1}^{p} a_k x[n-k] \qquad (3.32)$$

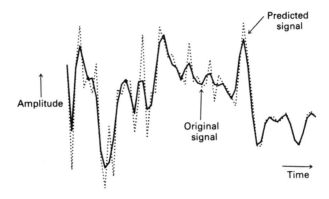

Figure 3.21   Graphical interpretation of linear prediction

where $\tilde{x}[n]$ is the predicted sample at instant n and $a_1, a_2, \ldots, a_p$ are the predictor coefficients. It will generally be impossible to predict each signal sample exactly and this leads to a prediction error $e[n]$ at each sample instant:

$$e[n] = x[n] - \tilde{x}[n] \tag{3.33}$$

By minimising the mean squared error between the actual speech samples and the linearly-predicted ones, the predictor coefficients (that is, the weighting coefficients of the linear combination) can be determined by solving a set of linear equations. A set of predictor coefficients can predict the speech signal reasonably accurately over stationary portions. In order to match the time-varying properties of the speech signal, a new set of predictor coefficients are calculated every 10–30 ms.

The problem in linear prediction is to determine the a_k coefficients so as to minimise the mean square error, E, over a specified number of samples. Now

$$E = \sum_n e^2[n] = \sum_n [x[n] - \tilde{x}[n]]^2 = \sum_n \left[x[n] - \sum_{k=1}^{p} a_k x[n-k]\right]^2 \tag{3.34}$$

The number of samples n over which the error is minimised is left unspecified for the moment.

If E is to be minimised by appropriate choice of the a_k coefficients, then the partial derivative of E with respect to each coefficient $a_j, j = 1, 2, \ldots, p$ should be zero, that is

$$\delta E/\delta a_j = -2\sum_n x[n-j] \cdot \left[x[n] - \sum_{k=1}^{p} a_k x[n-k]\right] = 0 \tag{3.35}$$

So

$$\sum_{k=1}^{p} a_k \sum_{n} x[n-j] \cdot x[n-k] = \sum_{n} x[n] \cdot x[n-j], j$$

$$= 1, 2, \ldots, p \qquad (3.36)$$

The above equation represents a set of p linear equations for the p unknowns a_k. Therefore, it should be possible to find a solution by matrix inversion. However, finding the solution to a system of equations in perhaps 10–15 unknowns is not a trivial problem even if the equations are linear! Fortunately, two different efficient methods exist for finding the solution of this system of equations. These are known as the *autocorrelation method* and the *covariance method*. Each will now be briefly described.

So far the limits of the summation in the expressions $\sum x[n-j] \cdot x[n-k]$ and $\sum x[n] \cdot x[n-j]$ in equation (3.36) have been left unspecified. Suppose initially that we assume that the signal is stationary with finite energy, which of course is not the case for speech, and the range of summation is from $-\infty$ to $+\infty$ with $x[n]$ being defined as zero for $n < 0$, then

$$\sum_{n=-\infty}^{\infty} x[n-j] \cdot x[n-k] = \sum_{n=-\infty}^{\infty} x[n-j+1] \cdot x[n-k+1] = \ldots$$

$$= \sum_{n=-\infty}^{\infty} x[n] \cdot x[n+j-k] \qquad (3.37)$$

Therefore the system of equations can be written as

$$\sum_{k=1}^{p} a_k \sum_{n=-\infty}^{\infty} x[n] \cdot x[n+j-k] = \sum_{n=-\infty}^{\infty} x[n] \cdot x[n-j], j = 1, 2, \ldots, p \qquad (3.38)$$

The multipliers of the a_k coefficients and the right-hand sides of the system of equations are in the form of autocorrelation values of the speech signal for specific time (sample) shifts. If $R(k)$ is defined as the autocorrelation value for a shift of k samples, that is

$$R(k) = \sum_{n=-\infty}^{\infty} x[n] \cdot x[n+k] \qquad (3.39)$$

the system of equations can be written as

$$\begin{bmatrix} R(0) & R(1) & R(2) & \ldots R(p-1) \\ R(1) & R(0) & R(1) & \ldots R(p-2) \\ R(2) & R(1) & R(0) & \ldots R(p-3) \\ \vdots & \vdots & \vdots & \vdots \\ R(p-1) & R(p-2) & R(p-3) & \ldots R(0) \end{bmatrix} \begin{bmatrix} a_1 \\ a_2 \\ a_3 \\ \vdots \\ a_p \end{bmatrix} = \begin{bmatrix} R(1) \\ R(2) \\ R(3) \\ \vdots \\ R(p) \end{bmatrix} \qquad (3.40)$$

This is a symmetric matrix and all diagonal elements are the same. It is known as a Toeplitz matrix and a very efficient method due to Durbin and Levinson [Markel and Gray, 1976] exists for solving this special system of equations. The Durbin–Levinson method requires much less computational effort than is generally needed for solving a system of linear equations. Of course, the speech signal is not known for all time and it is impossible and impractical to compute the infinite summations required to obtain the autocorrelation values. In addition, it is necessary to re-calculate a new set of coefficients, a_k, every 10–30 ms to reflect the changing nature of the speech signal, and hence short-time autocorrelation values are used. These are computed by first multiplying the speech signal $x[n]$ by a soft window function, $W[n]$ (for example, a Hamming window), of duration N samples (figure 3.22(a)) and the autocorrelation values are calculated from

$$R(k) = \sum_{n=0}^{N-1} \{W[n] \cdot x[n]\} \cdot \{W[n + k] \cdot x[n + k]\},$$

$$k = 0, 1, 2, \ldots, p \qquad (3.41)$$

In speech analysis this method of computing the predictor coefficients has become known as the *autocorrelation method* because of the presence of autocorrelation values in the system of equations for solving the predictor coefficients. Typically, a window of duration 20–30 ms (200 samples at a 10 kHz rate) is used and overlapping of adjacent windows is normally used to give an overall frame rate in the range 10–20 ms. A soft window function is essential in order to reduce the prediction error at the beginning and end of the segment. Large prediction errors will arise at the start of the interval ($0 \leqslant n \leqslant p - 1$) since the predictor is effectively being required to predict the signal from samples which have arbitrarily been set to zero, while at the end of the interval ($N \leqslant n \leqslant N + p - 1$) it is endeavouring to predict zero signal from samples that are non-zero.

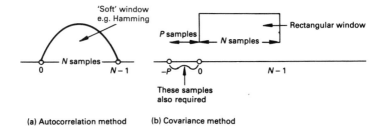

Figure 3.22   Illustration of analysis intervals for autocorrelation and covariance methods

In the *covariance method* of linear prediction, the system of equations for obtaining the predictor coefficients is set up in a slightly different way. Instead of adopting the initial premise of assuming a finite-energy signal and attempting to minimise the mean squared error over all time, a rectangular window is used to split the speech signal into segments and the error is minimised over each segment of length N. This leads to the following system of equations:

$$\sum_{k=1}^{p} a_k \sum_{n=0}^{N-1} x[n - j] \cdot x[n - k] = \sum_{n=0}^{N-1} x[n] \cdot x[n - j], j = 1, 2, \ldots, p \quad (3.42)$$

The multipliers of the predictor coefficients are not now true short-time autocorrelation values though they are computed in a similar way and are in the form of covariance values of the speech signal. The system of equations can be written more compactly as

$$\{Q(j, k)\} \cdot \{a_k\} = \{Q(j, 0)\}, j = 1, 2, \ldots, p \quad (3.43)$$

where

$$Q(k, j) = \sum_{n=0}^{N-1} x[n - j] \cdot x[n - k] \text{ and}$$

$$Q(j, 0) = \sum_{n=0}^{N-1} x[n] \cdot x[n - j] \quad (3.44)$$

Note that p sample values of $x[n]$ outside the range $0 \leqslant n \leqslant N - 1$ are required in computing the covariance matrix. This is illustrated in figure 3.22(b). Now $Q(j, k) = Q(k, j)$, that is the matrix is symmetrical about the main diagonal though all diagonal elements are not equal as for the autocorrelation matrix. The a_k coefficients of the predictor can be found by matrix inversion which is substantially easier for diagonally symmetric matrices because use can be made of a special technique called 'Cholesky's Theorem' which allows the matrix $Q(j, k)$ to be decomposed into the form $Q(j, k) = LL^T$ where L is a lower triangular matrix and L^T is its transpose. This leads to an efficient solution of the equations.

The covariance method does not use soft-windowing of the speech signal and as a result can give accurate estimates of prediction coefficients using a narrower window than in the autocorrelation method. Unlike the autocorrelation method, however, it is not always guaranteed to produce a stable predictor. Typically, speech samples covering a period of 10 ms (100 samples at a 10 kHz rate) would be used. A new set of coefficients would normally be calculated every 10–30 ms without any overlap of adjacent windows.

The previous discussion on linear prediction shows that it is essentially a time-domain waveform coding technique which allows perhaps 100–200 samples of a speech signal to be represented by about 10–15 coefficients. However, once the predictor coefficients are known they can also be used to estimate the vocal tract response.

The error signal $e[n]$ is easily computed using the predictor coefficients since it follows from equations (3.32) and (3.33) that

$$e[n] = x[n] - \sum_{k=1}^{p} a_k x[n - k]$$

$$= x[n] - a_1 x[n - 1] - a_2 x[n - 2] - \ldots - a_p x[n - p] \quad (3.45)$$

If the error signal, $e[n]$, is known, it is possible to reconstruct the original signal $x[n]$ exactly from the predicted signal $\tilde{x}[n]$, that is

$$x[n] = e[n] + \tilde{x}[n] = e[n] + \sum_{k=1}^{p} a_k x[n - k] \quad (3.46)$$

Taking z-transforms gives

$$X(z) = E(z) + \left[\sum_{k=1}^{p} a_k z^{-k} \right] X(z)$$

$$X(z) = E(z) \Big/ \left(1 - \sum_{k=1}^{p} a_k z^{-k}\right) = H(z) \cdot E(z) \quad (3.47)$$

where $X(z)$ and $E(z)$ are the z-transforms of $x[n]$ and $e[n]$ respectively and

$$H(z) = 1 \Big/ \left(1 - \sum_{k=1}^{p} a_k z^{-k}\right) \quad (3.48)$$

is the transfer function of a digital system or filter which contains only powers of z in its denominator and for this reason is often referred to as an all-pole system. (The 'poles' are the roots of the denominator polynomial in z.) From a systems viewpoint, equation (3.47) shows that the speech signal $x[n]$ may be viewed as the output of this all-pole filter when the input is the error signal $e[n]$. The filter $H(z)$ therefore models the vocal tract response and $e[n]$ denotes the vocal tract excitation. An estimate of the vocal tract spectral envelope, $H(\omega)$, may be obtained by putting $z = e^{j\omega T}$ in the transfer function $H(z)$ of the all-pole linear predictor, that is

$$|H(\omega)| = \left| 1 \Big/ \left(1 - \sum_{k=1}^{p} a_k e^{-j\omega kT}\right) \right| \quad (3.49)$$

The spectrum is obtained by evaluating $|H(\omega)|$ at various values of ω in the above equation. Figure 3.23 shows the linear prediction spectrum of a 20 ms

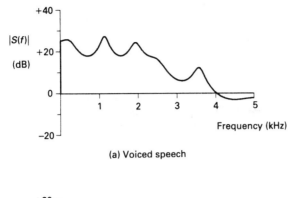

(a) Voiced speech

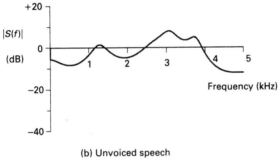

(b) Unvoiced speech

Figure 3.23   Typical short-time linear prediction spectrum

segment of voiced speech taken from the vowel /a/. The autocorrelation method was used to compute the coefficients of a 12th-order linear predictor. A Hamming window was used to multiply the speech segment prior to the analysis. The spectrum is clearly very smooth and exhibits no harmonic ripple due to pitch. The formant structure of the vowel is clearly apparent. Although the computed linear prediction spectrum will not match exactly the true spectrum of the speech signal, it is a very close approximation.

The process of minimising the mean squared error between the original speech samples and the linearly predicted ones tends to produce an error signal which has a broadly flat or 'white' spectrum. The degree of 'whiteness' in the error spectrum depends on how good the predictor is in modelling the signal. For voiced speech, the error signal is a periodic pulse-like signal at pitch frequency (figure 3.24(a)). The peaks in the signal occur at points corresponding to glottal closure when the amplitude of the speech signal reaches a maximum. At these points the predictor finds it more difficult to model the speech signal. At points other than glottal closure, when the vocal tract is in force-free oscillation, the predictor is able to model the signal very well and the prediction error is small. For an

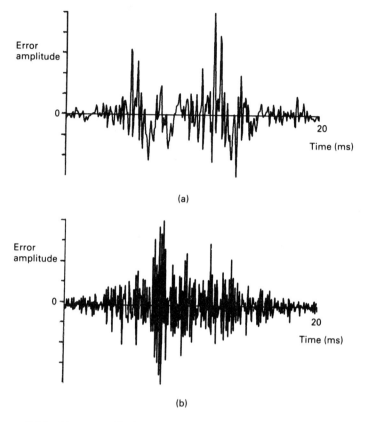

Figure 3.24 Linear prediction error signal for voiced and unvoiced speech

ideal predictor, the error signal would consist of an impulse train at pitch frequency which has an exactly flat or white spectrum. In the case of unvoiced speech, minimisation of the mean squared error results in an error signal which is close to white noise which again has a flat spectrum (figure 3.24(b)).

As we have already been, the error signal $e[n]$ is easily computed using the predictor coefficients. From equation (3.47):

$$E(z) = \frac{1}{H(z)} \cdot X(z) = A(z) \cdot X(z) \tag{3.50}$$

where

$$A(z) = \frac{1}{H(z)} = \left\{ 1 - \sum_{k=1}^{p} a_k z^{-k} \right\} \tag{3.51}$$

Thus the error signal may be viewed as being obtained when the original speech signal $x[n]$ is processed through an all-zero digital filter $A(z)$ which is the inverse of the all-pole filter $H(z)$. (An all-zero filter has only powers of z in the denominator of its transfer function and the zeros are the roots of the numerator polynomial.) For obvious reasons, the process of obtaining the error signal is often referred to as *inverse filtering*.

The main attraction of linear predictive analysis is that it offers great accuracy and speed of computation. In addition, the theory underlying the method has been the subject of intensive research in recent years and, as a result, is highly developed and well understood. Based on this theory, a large variety and range of applications of linear predictive analysis to speech processing have evolved. Schemes have been devised for estimating all the basic speech parameters from linear predictive analysis, such as spectrum and formant estimation, pitch detection and glottal pulse shape estimation. Some of these will be discussed in the next chapter.

The main drawback with linear predictive analysis is that an all-pole model is used to approximate the vocal tract transfer function. As might be expected, this type of analysis is capable of describing reasonably well the transfer function during non-nasal vowel and vowel-like sounds. However, a general transfer function of a real vocal tract has both poles and zeros in its transfer function and therefore an accurate analysis or synthesis model of speech production should be of the pole–zero type. This is particularly true in the case of sounds like nasals and stops and indeed to account for any zeros present in the source-spectrum. When zeros are introduced into the model for linear predictive analysis, many of the convenient properties of the method have to be abandoned. The main problem is that there is a requirement to solve a system of non-linear equations which involves an iterative process rather than a simple matrix inversion.

3.8 Pitch-synchronous analysis

A drawback of any speech analysis technique that involves carrying out the analysis over a few tens of milliseconds or a few pitch-periods is that an averaging process occurs, particularly where the spectrum is changing rapidly, with consequent 'blurring' of rapidly varying spectral properties. Also in this type of pitch-asynchronous analysis, the computed spectrum is the product of the excitation spectrum and the vocal tract spectrum and the two are not readily separated. Thus the effect is to 'distort' the vocal tract spectral envelope. This is particularly noticeable if the excitation spectrum has anti-resonances (zeros) near the resonances (poles) of the vocal tract.

Both of these problems may be overcome by a pitch-synchronous analysis in which single pitch-periods of the speech signal are identified and analysed in isolation. In order to eliminate the effects of glottal pulse shape

68   *Signal Processing of Speech*

the analysis should be carried out over closed-glottis regions where the vocal tract is in force-free oscillation. The main drawback with any type of pitch-synchronous analysis is that it is difficult to identify accurately and automatically the start and finish of each pitch-period and the closed-glottis region within each pitch-period.

Problems

3.1. A digital pre-emphasis filter is described by the difference equation

$$y[n] = x[n] - 0.95\, x[n-1]$$

Compute the output of the filter for the input sequence 0, 2, 1, −2, −3, 0, 1, 0, 0, . . . , 0, ... Assume the signal is zero prior to $t = 0$.

3.2. A simple digital bandpass filter is described by the difference equation

$$y[n] = x[n] - 0.25y[n-1] + 0.5y[n-2]$$

(a) Draw a block diagram of the filter.
(b) Compute the first five samples of the output when the input is a unit-sample applied at $t = 0$, that is $x[n] = 1, 0, 0, 0, \ldots$. Assume that $y[n-1] = y[n-2] = 0$ prior to $t = 0$.

3.3. Show that applying the bilinear transformation (equation (3.6)) to the s-domain bandpass transfer function of equation (3.11) produces a digital filter with a z-domain transfer function specified by equations (3.12) and (3.13). Draw the block diagram of the filter.

3.4. Using the bilinear tranformation, design a second-order Butterworth low-pass digital filter with a cut-off frequency of 3.3 kHz. The s-domain transfer function of the prototype analogue filter is

$$H(s) = \frac{\omega_c^2}{s^2 + \sqrt{2}\omega_c s + \omega_c^2}$$

where ω_c is the cut-off frequency of the filter in radians/s. Derive the difference equation of the filter and draw its block diagram.

3.5. An N-term 'moving-average' filter is an FIR filter in which all of the filter coefficients are equal to $1/N$ and, as its name suggests, is used to compute the average value of a signal over time. Draw the structure of a 5-term moving-average filter and calculate the filter output sequence for the input sequence 3, 5, −2, −3, 1, −4, 2, 1. Assume that the filter delay elements contain zeros prior to the application of the first input sample. Determine the output of the filter when the input is a unit sample sequence, that is $x[n] = 1, 0, 0, \ldots, 0, \ldots$ Comment on the result.

3.6. A fast Fourier transform (FFT) algorithm is to be used to compute the discrete Fourier transform (DFT) of a speech signal at 10 ms time intervals. Assuming a speech sample rate 10 kHz, calculate a suitable number of points for the FFT analysis and the corresponding spacing in Hz between adjacent frequency components in the short-time spectrum.

3.7. Calculate the discrete Fourier transform of the 8-point sequence $x[n]$ $= 1, 2, -1, -2, 0, 1, 2, 0$, using
   (i) the direct DFT (equation (3.22))
   (ii) the FFT algorithm depicted in figure 3.16.

3.8. Calculate the autocorrelation function of the discrete time signal $x[n]$ in problem 3.7.

4 Feature Extraction

In the previous chapter, a number of parametric, short-time speech analysis techniques, such as filter banks, discrete/fast Fourier transform, cepstral analysis, autocorrelation and linear predictive analysis, were described. In all of these methods, speech is analysed in 10–30 ms time frames and for each frame, a set of parameters or coefficients is derived which either directly or indirectly yields information about the vocal tract and/or its excitation function, and also characterises the speech waveform itself.

In this chapter, the topic of speech analysis is extended to include the extraction of features which are directly associated with speech production. The main topics to be considered are formant frequency and pitch frequency estimation and segmentation of the speech into identifiable phonetic units. The chapter begins, however, with a description of techniques for determining the short-time energy function of the speech signal, its zero-crossing rate and where it begins and ends (endpoint detection). The important topic of vector quantisation is also covered.

4.1 Short-time energy function

The short-time energy function of speech may be computed by splitting the speech signal into frames of N samples and computing the total squared values of the signal samples in each frame. Splitting the signal into frames can be achieved by multiplying the signal by a suitable window $W[n]$, $n = 0, 1, 2, \ldots, N - 1$, which is zero for n outside the range $(0, N - 1)$. A simple rectangular window of duration 10–20 ms is suitable for this purpose. For a window starting at sample m, the short-time energy function E_m may be written as

$$E_m = \sum_n \{x[n] \cdot W[n-m]\}^2 \tag{4.1}$$

A simpler function which is sometimes used to extract a measure related to energy is the short-time magnitude function defined as

$$W[m] = \sum_n |x[n]| \cdot W[n-m] \tag{4.2}$$

A plot of the short-time energy function of a segment of speech contain-

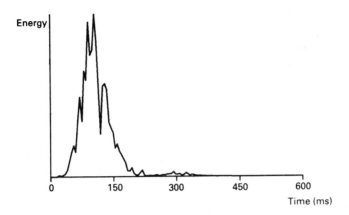

Figure 4.1   Short-time energy function for a segment of voiced/unvoiced speech

ing both voiced and unvoiced speech is shown in figure 4.1. The energy of voiced speech is generally greater than that of unvoiced speech though there are occasions when the energy of strong fricatives is greater than that of weak vowels.

4.2 Zero-crossing rate

Zero-crossing rate is a measure of the number of times in a given time interval (frame) that the amplitude of the speech signal passes through a value of zero. Plots of zero-crossing rate for segments of voiced and unvoiced speech are given in figure 4.2. Because of its random nature, the

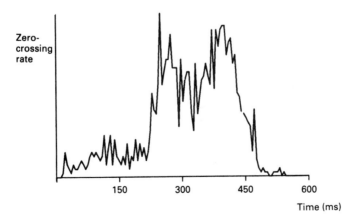

Figure 4.2   Zero-crossing rate for a segment of voiced/unvoiced speech

zero-crossing rate for unvoiced speech is greater than that of voiced speech. Zero-crossing rate is an important parameter for voiced/unvoiced classification and for endpoint detection. It is also often used as part of the front-end processing in automatic speech recognition systems.

4.3 Endpoint detection

One of the most basic but problematic aspects of speech processing is to detect when a speech utterance begins and ends. This is often referred to as endpoint detection. Endpointing is particularly difficult to do accurately, if the speech is uttered in a noisy environment. In the case of unvoiced (noisy) sounds occurring at the beginning or end of an utterance, it is difficult to distinguish accurately the speech signal from the background noise signal.

Many pitch detection algorithms are based on measurement of the signal short-time energy and zero-crossing rate and attempt to detect as accurately as possible the changes that these quantities undergo at the beginning and end of an utterance. The basic operation of a simple algorithm is as follows. A small sample of the background noise is taken during a 'silence' interval just prior to the commencement of the speech signal. The short-time energy function of the entire utterance is then computed using equation (4.1) or (4.2). A speech threshold is determined which takes into account the silence energy and the peak energy. Initially, the endpoints are assumed to occur where the signal energy crosses this threshold. Corrections to these initial estimates are then made by computing the zero crossing-rate in the vicinity of the endpoints and by comparing it with that of the 'silence'. If detectable changes in zero-crossing rate occur outside the initial thresholds, the endpoints are re-designated to the points at which the changes take place.

4.4 Vector quantisation

As we have already seen in the previous chapter, in most parametric speech analysis techniques, speech is analysed in a sequence of time frames and each frame is represented by a set of k numerical values, for example 16 filter bank outputs, 12 LPC coefficients etc. Thus each frame is represented by a k-dimensional vector in a k-dimensional space. Normally each parameter in the vector is quantised separately using a specific number of bits. This is referred to as scalar quantisation. It may not be the most economical method of quantisation since it implies that the speech frames are expected to occur uniformly throughout the vector space. In many speech processing applications such as speech coding (chapter 6) and speech recognition (chapter 7), it is often more economical or more convenient to use a different form of parameter quantisation called vector quantisation.

The basic idea of vector quantisation is that the vector space is divided up into a number, N, of non-uniform regions or bins, with each region being represented by a single vector giving the centroid of the bin. The collection of N vector centroids is referred to as a codebook and each element of the codebook is given a unique label or address. The process of vector quantisation is illustrated in figure 4.3 for a two-dimensional vector space in which each frame is represented by a point in the X–Y co-ordinate system. The centroid of each bin is indicated by a '+' which represents all vectors in that bin. In the actual process of vector quantisation, the input vector V to be quantised is assigned to the nearest bin. This is achieved by comparing the distance d between the input vector V with all of the vector centroids $\bar{V}_i$ and choosing the one for which the distance is smallest. If $d(V-\bar{V}_i)$ denotes the distance between any two vectors, then the address of the quantised vector A_q is given by

$$A_q = \operatorname*{Argmin}_{i} [d(V - \bar{V}_i)] \tag{4.3}$$

where Argmin denotes the value of the index or address i for which the expression inside the square brackets is a minimum.

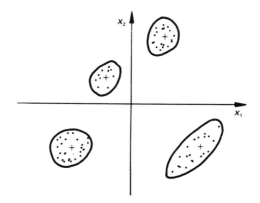

Figure 4.3 Illustration of vector quantisation (2 dimensions)

For spectral vectors, such as filter bank outputs, FFT spectra etc., the metric that is often used in computing the distance $d(V_1, V_2)$ between two k-dimensional vectors is the Euclidean distance defined as

$$d(V_1, V_2) = |V_1 - V_2|^2 = \sum_{i=1}^{k} (V_1(i) - V_2(i))^2 \tag{4.4}$$

which is the sum of the squared differences of the elements in the two vectors. In the case of LPC vectors, a more suitable metric is the Itakura distance measure which is defined as

$$d(V_1, V_2) = a_1^T R_1 a_1 / a_2^T R_2 a_2 \qquad (4.5)$$

where a_1 and a_2 and R_1 and R_2 are the coefficient vectors and the autocorrelation matrices corresponding to the vectors V_1 and V_2 and a_1^T and a_2^T denote vector transposes. Since the metric is non-symmetric, that is $d(V_1, V_2)$ is not equal to $d(V_2, V_1)$, it is common practice to use $1/2\{d(V_1, V_2) + d(V_2, V_1)\}$ for calculating the distance between the two vectors V_1 and V_2.

A very important aspect of any vector quantisation scheme is the provision of an adequate number of training vectors and the processing of these to produce an optimal bin structure for the vector space. One popular algorithm for codebook design is the so-called LBG algorithm whose name derives from the first letters of the three researchers who developed it – Linde, Buzo and Gray. The starting point for this algorithm is some initial estimate of the codebook. There are a number of ways of obtaining this initial estimate. One method is to quantise the vector space uniformly into the specified number of bins N and then calculate the centroid of each bin. An alternative method is simply to take the first N vectors of the training sequence. Once the initial codebook has been established, training using the LBG algorithm proceeds by calculating the distance between each element in the training sequence with each initial codebook centroid, then assigning each vector to the nearest bin and calculating new centroids for each bin. The training sequence is once again compared with the new codebook as before and if the codebook distortion, computed by summing the distances between the vectors allocated to each bin and the bin centroid across all the bins, is sufficiently better than the previous distortion figure, the complete training sequence is once again used to further adjust the codebook as before. This process is repeated until the reduction in distortion falls below a pre-determined threshold value. A slight variation on this algorithm is to combine each vector of the training sequence individually with its nearest bin by working out a new bin centroid as each training vector is presented.

4.5 Formant tracking

The formant frequencies, amplitudes and, to a lesser extent, bandwidths of the vocal tract are extremely important features, since their values characterise individual speech sounds. The estimation of formant parameters or formant tracking is therefore a very important aspect of speech processing. Since formants are manifested as peaks in the short-time amplitude spectrum $|X(k)|$, it might seem at first that all that is required in each analysis frame is a simple peak-picking algorithm which identifies a peak at the kth spectral point if

$$|X(k-1)| < |X(k)| > |X(k+1)| \tag{4.6}$$

and labels the formants by assigning F_1 to the lowest-frequency peak, F_2 to the next highest-frequency peak and so on until four or five formants have been assigned. Unfortunately, for a wide variety of reasons, this simple approach will almost certainly produce incorrect formant tracking. It is impossible to be certain that all the peaks in the short-time spectrum correspond to formants or indeed that genuine formants are not being masked in one way or another. Unless pitch-synchronous analysis has been employed, the short-time amplitude spectrum of speech contains spectral information about the excitation source as well as the vocal tract itself and clearly in formant-tracking the vocal tract response only is of interest.

The contribution due to the excitation is particularly noticeable when a narrowband DFT or FFT analysis is carried out. With this type of analysis (see figure 3.11), the harmonics of the excitation are clearly evident. Such a spectrum can be smoothed, by treating the spectral values as a time-series and by passing them through a low-pass filter. In order to correct for possible shifting of the position of the spectral peaks due to the filtering action (equivalent to a time-delay in a time-domain signal), the smoothed spectrum is normally filtered again in the reverse direction; in other words the order in which the spectral values are presented to the filter is the reverse of the first filtering operation. This second filtering action has a further smoothing effect and in fact the complete bipass filtering operation can be repeated a number of times (multi-pass filtering).

A number of spectral analysis techniques yield inherently smooth short-time spectra, which are relatively free from the ripple effects of the pitch harmonics but nevertheless are still multiplied by the spectral envelope of the excitation. Cepstrally-smoothed (figure 3.18) and linear prediction (figure 3.23) spectra are in this category and little can be gained by any further processing. Filter bank spectra may be suitable for obtaining formant frequencies, provided that there is a sufficient number of channels to provide adequate frequency resolution. Unless particular care is taken with the choice of the filter analysing bandwidths, filter bank spectra will normally require some form of spectral smoothing.

From frame to frame, even smoothed short-time spectra will almost certainly exhibit spurious spectral peaks. Some of these may be attributed to artefacts of the analysis process, since no speech analysis technique is ideal. At times, two formant frequencies may come very close together and are not individually resolved by the analysis process and so appear as a single broadband peak. Certain consonants, such as nasals, exhibit anti-resonances (zeros) close to the resonances (poles) of the vocal tract, which cause the amplitude of the formant to be reduced and sometimes masked entirely. Sometimes, zeros in the excitation spectrum can occur in the vicinity of the first formant and this can split the formant into two distinct peaks, thereby introducing an apparent extra formant.

In the case of linear prediction, there exists a more accurate, though computationally more expensive, method for formant estimation. Instead of peak-picking in the short-time amplitude spectrum, the poles of the prediction filter are computed and these are related to the formant frequencies and bandwidths of the vocal tract. The predictor filter has a transfer function given by equation (3.40) and the poles may be computed by equating the denominator to zero, that is

$$1 - \sum_{k=1}^{P} a_k z^{-k} = 0 \quad \text{or} \quad \sum_{k=1}^{P} a_k z^{-k} = 1 \tag{4.7}$$

The above equation has p roots $\{z_k\}$ which may be either real or complex. If they are complex, they occur in complex conjugate pairs. The z-plane roots z_k are related to the s-plane roots s_k through the equation

$$z_k = e^{s_k T} \tag{4.8}$$

where $s_k = \sigma_k + j\omega_k$, ω_k being the radian frequency of the kth pole and σ_k being equal to half its bandwidth. It follows therefore that the frequency f_k and bandwidth b_k, in Hz, of the z-plane root z_k are given by the equations

$$f_k = \frac{1}{2\pi T} \text{Imag}\{\log_e[z_k]\} \tag{4.9a}$$

and

$$b_k = \frac{1}{\pi T} \text{Real}\{\log_e[z_k]\} \tag{4.9b}$$

The pole frequencies generally correspond directly to the formant frequencies, though on occasions, certain formants are missing from the pole frequencies and some poles do not correspond to any formant. Like all formant estimation procedures, some further processing is required, which normally involves examining the frame-to-frame variation of the pole frequencies (or the frequencies of the spectral peaks) before formants are identified and labelled. Figure 4.4 illustrates the type of data that results after calculating the pole frequencies, or after determining the frequencies of the spectral peaks, for individual frames of an utterance. The data are plotted on a frequency–time graph, in which a peak in a particular time-

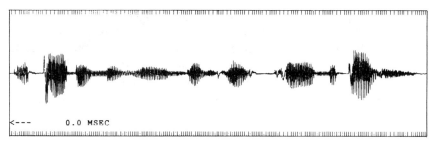

(a) Speech signal

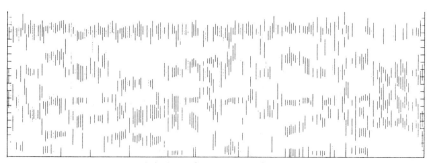

(b) Raw formant tracks

(c) Smoothed formant tracks

Figure 4.4   Example of formant tracking

frame (horizontal axis) is indicated by a short line segment plotted at its frequency value in the vertical direction. The centre of each vertical line segment indicates the formant frequency value and the extremities give the −3 dB bandwidth positions. The purpose of an automatic formant tracking algorithm is to derive the formant tracks by obtaining smooth continuous paths through this type of data. A number of algorithms of varying complexities have been developed to tackle this problem. Possibly the simplest is one in which the spectral frequency range is restricted to the 0–3 kHz band and an attempt is made to identify three formants in this region. If exactly three peaks are found, then these are assigned to the formants. It has been reported that, in the case of male speech, this occurs approximately 85–90 per cent of the time. In order to handle the other possible eventualities, that is one, two, or more peaks, a nearest-neighbour criterion is employed. This involves computing the distances $d(i, j)$ between each candidate frequency in the current frame k, $f_i(k)$, and each formant frequency assigned in the previous frame, $F_j(k-1)$. Mathematically this is written as

$$d(i, j) = |f_i(k) - F_j(k-1)|, \quad \begin{matrix} i = 1, 2, \ldots, N_P \\ j = 1, 2, 3 \end{matrix} \qquad (4.10)$$

where $|\;|$ denotes the magnitude function and N_P is the number of peaks (pole frequencies) found in the current frame. When one peak is found, its formant label is assigned as the nearest formant neighbour from the previous frame and the two vacant formant slots are filled with their values in the previous frame. When two peaks are found, their formant labels are assigned in accordance with the nearest-neighbour criterion as before and the missing formant assumes its value in the previous frame. In the case of four or more peaks, the three peaks closest to the formant values of the previous are identified and labelled and the remainder are discarded.

The simple algorithm described above works from left to right, using the formant values of the previous frame to resolve any difficulty or ambiguity in assigning formant values in the current frame. More sophisticated algorithms have been developed, which operate from right to left as well as left to right. These identify clear regions of strong formant structure (anchor points) in the data, and formant tracking is carried out in both directions from these anchor points. Some algorithms use additional processing to resolve closely-spaced formants and place restrictions on the degree to which formants can move between one frame and another. It is also possible to use techniques such as dynamic programming and neural networks to obtain smooth formant tracks.

4.6 Pitch extraction

The estimation of the fundamental frequency or pitch-period of the excitation source is another important aspect of speech analysis. Pitch estimation is almost always an essential requirement in systems for pitch-synchronous analysis (section 3.8), speech analysis/synthesis (section 5.5) and speech coding (chapter 6). It may also prove to be of benefit in automatic speech recognition and speaker identification/verification (chapter 7), though to date, pitch information has not played a significant role in these systems.

Pitch extraction algorithms can operate either directly on the time-waveform (time-domain algorithms) or on the spectrum of the speech signal (frequency-domain algorithms). The main principles of a number of these algorithms will be described in the following sub-sections.

4.6.1 Gold–Rabiner pitch extractor [Gold and Rabiner, 1969]

A visual examination of the time-waveform of voiced speech (for example figure 1.4(a)) often reveals its periodic nature with the principal peaks in the waveform corresponding to maximum points of excitation of the vocal tract, as the vocal cords close rapidly. It would seem therefore that an algorithm which accurately located the position of these principal peaks might form the basis of a scheme for estimating pitch. Such an algorithm would normally start by low-pass filtering the speech signal to a bandwidth of approximately 1 kHz. This removes much of the high-frequency information and yields a much smoother waveform. However, such a simple system will often make incorrect estimates of pitch, since the maximum point of excitation is not always directly determinable from the time waveform. The development of the Gold–Rabiner algorithm was based on a recognition of this fact and, as well as detecting the peak signal values, it uses additional features of the time-waveform to obtain a number of parallel estimates of the pitch-period. The final pitch estimate is determined as the best overall consensus of a total of six pitch estimates. The main waveform features used by the algorithm are illustrated in figure 4.5. These are six positive pulse trains $m_1(n)$ to $m_6(n)$, where:

m_1 = the magnitude of the current peak amplitude;
m_2 = the magnitude of the difference in amplitude between the current peak and the previous valley;
m_3 = the magnitude of the difference in amplitude between the current peak and the previous peak;
m_4 = the magnitude of the current valley amplitude;
m_5 = the magnitude of the difference in amplitude between the current valley amplitude and the previous peak amplitude;
m_6 = the magnitude of the difference between the current valley amplitude and the previous valley amplitude.

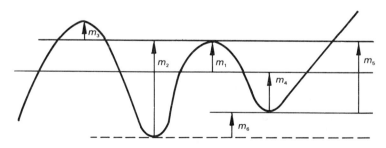

Figure 4.5   Features used in Gold–Rabiner pitch extractor

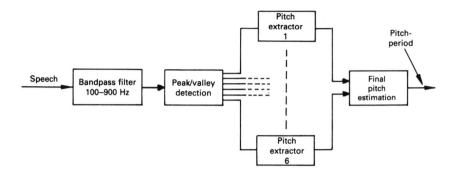

Figure 4.6   Block diagram of Gold–Rabiner pitch extractor

A block diagram illustrating the complete Gold–Rabiner algorithm is shown in figure 4.6. After being bandpass-filtered using a filter with lower and upper cut-off frequencies of 100 Hz and 900 Hz respectively, the speech signal is fed to the peak–valley detection module, which detects a peak in the signal $x(n)$, if $x[n-1]< x[n] > x[n + 1]$ and a valley if $x[n-1]> x[n] < x[n + 1]$. The output of this module is the six pulse trains $m_1[n]$–$m_6[n]$, computed as described above, which are then fed to six separate but identical pitch extractors.

The operation of each pitch extractor is illustrated in figure 4.7. A pulse detector operates on the input pulse train and when a pulse is detected, a blanking interval is activated, during which no pulses are detected. Following the end of the blanking interval, a decaying envelope is started, which decays exponentially from the amplitude of the previously detected pulse, until a pulse whose amplitude exceeds that of the envelope is detected. The

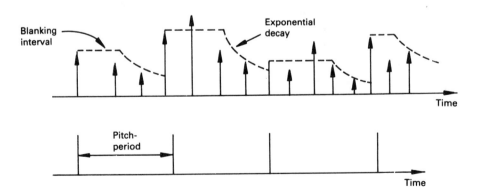

Figure 4.7   Illustration of individual pitch estimator in Gold–Rabiner algorithm

value of the envelope is then set to the amplitude of the newly detected pulse and the process is repeated. The new pitch period estimate T_{new} is the time interval between successively detected pulses.

The blanking interval time t_b and the time-constant τ of the exponential decay are computed in proportion to the current average estimate of the pitch period T_{av}. The current value of $T_{av}[m]$ is computed from the previous value $T_{av}[m-1]$, using the relationship

$$T_{av}[m] = 0.5[T_{av}[m-1] + T_{new}] \qquad (4.11)$$

The values of t_b and τ are computed from T_{av} using the equations

$$t_b = K_1 T_{av} \quad \text{and} \quad \tau = K_2 T_{av} \qquad (4.12)$$

where K_1 and K_2 are constants. Optimum values of K_1 and K_2 have been determined experimentally to be 0.4 and 1.44 respectively.

The six pitch-period estimates are then fed to the final pitch estimation module. The pitch estimate in each channel, i, is expanded to generate six possible pitch candidates – the current pitch estimate, T_{i1}, the two previous pitch estimates T_{i2} and T_{i3} and three further estimates, T_{i4}, T_{i5} and T_{i6}, which are formed by adding combinations of the current and previous estimates. Specifically

$$T_{i4} = T_{i1} + T_{i2}, \quad T_{i5} = T_{i2} + T_{i3} \quad \text{and} \quad T_{i6} = T_{i1} + T_{i2} + T_{i3}$$

The formation of the last three estimates perhaps seem a little odd. This is done in order to take account of the possible identification of false peaks. If any of the peaks leading to the estimates T_{i1}, T_{i2} or T_{i3} have been falsely identified, then the actual pitch period could be T_{i4}, T_{i5} or T_{i6}. This generates a total of 36 pitch candidates which are stored in a (6×6) matrix. Each element in the matrix is compared with every other element and the number of elements that are sufficiently close are labelled. The element with the greatest total of sufficiently close elements is selected as the current pitch estimate. A voiced/unvoiced decision is based on the values of the six most recent estimates of pitch. The complete process is repeated at 5 ms time intervals.

4.6.2 Autocorrelation methods

A number of pitch detection algorithms are based on computing the short-time autocorrelation function of the speech signal. The speech is normally low-pass filtered at a frequency of about 1 kHz, which is well above the maximum anticipated frequency range for pitch (500–600 Hz for female speech). Filtering helps to reduce the effects of the higher formants and any extraneous high-frequency noise. Because of the reduced band-width, a sample rate of about 2 kHz can be used. If the speech has been originally sampled at a higher rate, it can be down-sampled after filtering. Then the signal is windowed, using an appropriate soft window (such as Hamming) of duration 20–30 ms and the autocorrelation function is calculated as described in section 3.6 (equation (3.31)). The window is then advanced by the frame duration, typically 10 ms, and the process is repeated. In the case of voiced speech, the main peak in short-time autocorrelation function normally occurs at a lag equal to the pitch-period (figure 3.20(a)). This peak is therefore detected and its time position gives the pitch-period of the input speech. In the case of unvoiced speech, the short-time autocorrelation function exhibits no strong peaks and overall has a much lower amplitude (figure 3.20(b)). A voiced/unvoiced decision can be made, at least partially, on the ratio of the amplitude of the main peak to the amplitude of the correlation function for zero time lag, that is $R(0)$. Typically if the amplitude of the main peak is less than $R(0)/4$, the speech frame is declared unvoiced, otherwise it is voiced. The short-time energy function and zero-crossing rate of the input signal may also be used to assist with the voiced/unvoiced decision (sections 4.1 and 4.2).

The most common errors made by the type of autocorrelation pitch estimator described above are those due to confusion between the pitch periodicity and the periodicity of the formants, particularly the first in the case of speech low-pass filtered with a cut-off around 1 kHz. The effects of the formants can be reduced by carrying out some simple non-linear operations on the signal prior to calculating the autocorrelation function. One of the simplest is to cube the signal or raise it to some other high, odd power. This enhances the high-amplitude parts of the waveform and suppresses the low-amplitude parts. The overall effect is to emphasise the high-amplitude periodic pitch component relative to the lower-amplitude formant components and reduces the risk of confusion in the autocorrelation function. Another approach is to 'centre-clip' the speech signal as illustrated in figure 4.8(a). This involves suppressing values of the signal between two adjustable clipping thresholds and retaining those values falling outside. The unsuppressed values are assigned a new zero reference value equal to the clipping thresholds. These are typically set at $\pm\frac{1}{3}$ of the maximum amplitude value. Centre-clipping removes most of the formant information, leaving substantial components due to the pitch periodicity (figure 4.8(b)), which shows up more clearly in the autocorrelation function.

Because of the computational intensity of the many multiplications required in the computation of the autocorrelation function, two techniques have been developed which eliminate the need for multiplication in autocorrelation-based algorithms. The first technique uses centre-clipped speech but applies tertiary (3-level) clipping. If the signal is greater than

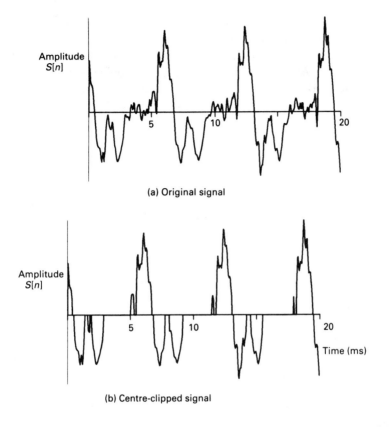

(a) Original signal

(b) Centre-clipped signal

Figure 4.8   Example of centre-clipped speech signal

the upper clipping threshold, it is assigned a value of 1; if it is less than the bottom threshold, it is assigned a value of -1. Suppressed signal values are assigned a value of 0. Multiplication then becomes a simple 1-bit ternary ANDing operation, with the only possible products being 1, -1 or 0. This significantly reduces the amount of computation and there is no significant degradation in performance.

The second approach to reducing the amount of computation involves using a modified version of the autocorrelation function which does not require the use of multiplications. This modified version is known as the *average magnitude difference function* (AMDF) and is given by

$$d(k) = \sum_{n=0}^{N-1} |x_\mathrm{w}[n] - x_\mathrm{w}[n+k]|, \qquad k = 0, 1, 2, \ldots \qquad (4.13)$$

where $x_\mathrm{w}[n]$ denotes the windowed input signal, N is the number of samples in the window and k is the lag index. A simple examination of the above equation indicates that when the time lag k is equal to the pitch-period of the input speech and the amplitude values of $x_w[n]$ and $x_w[n + k]$ are very similar, the AMDF will exhibit a valley as opposed to a peak for the autocorrelation function. This is the only essential difference between the AMDF and the autocorrelation function and, with the exception that valleys rather than peaks are being detected, it can be used in an identical way for pitch estimation.

4.6.3 The SIFT algorithm [Markel, 1972]

As already discussed in section 3.7, the linear prediction error signal (figure 3.24) resembles a real vocal-tract excitation signal, being a periodic pulse train at pitch frequency for voiced speech and a random-noise signal in the case of unvoiced speech. It is apparent therefore that derivation of the *LPC* residual signal would be a useful first step in a pitch-detection algorithm based on the autocorrelation method described in the previous section. This is precisely the basic operation of the *simplified inverse filter tracking* (SIFT) algorithm to be described in this section.

A diagram showing the main processing blocks in the SIFT algorithm is given in figure 4.9. It is assumed that the input speech signal has already been sampled at a 10 kHz rate. The algorithm was designed to estimate the pitch of male speech in the range 50–250 Hz. To simplify the LPC analysis, the signal is low-pass filtered with a cut-off of 800 Hz (a 3-pole, 2 dB Chebychev filter is used) and down-sampled to 2 kHz by selecting every fifth sample. The speech signal is pre-emphasised, using a simple differencing operation and then a fourth-order LPC analysis is carried out. This reduced-order predictor is adequate here because of the band-limiting of the input speech and the fourth-order predictor provides the two pole-pairs required to model the maximum of two formants which might be expected to occur in the range 0–1 kHz. Typically, the speech signal is windowed, using an 80-point (40 ms) window, which is advanced at 10 ms time intervals. In this case, a *Hanning window* is used. This is similar in form to the Hamming window encountered in section 3.2 but has the slightly different equation $\{W(n) = 0.5 - 0.5\cos(2\pi n/N), 0 \leqslant n \leqslant N\}$. A 40 ms window is normally expected to contain a minimum of two pitch-periods. The calculated predictor coefficients define the transfer function of the time-varying inverse filter $A(z)$ which filters the band-limited speech to produce the error signal $e[n]$. Next, the autocorrelation function of the error signal is computed. Again a Hanning window is used with the window durations and frame times typically the same as before.

In the pitch estimation module, the strongest peak in the autocorrelation function that occurs in the anticipated time-lag range, that is 4–20 ms (250–50 Hz), is found. In practice, the last pitch estimate is used to restrict the search region to within a narrow region either side of its value. Because of the relatively low sample rate of 2 kHz, the pitch resolution is limited to

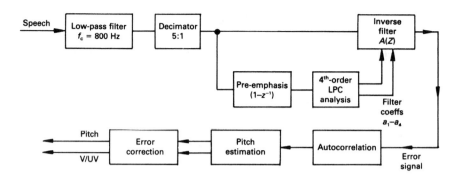

Figure 4.9 Block diagram of SIFT algorithm

0.5 ms, which is quite coarse. In order to overcome this, a form of parabolic interpolation is used to interpolate the autocorrelation function in the vicinity of the peak, in order to determine its location more accurately. A variable threshold is used, with the threshold level increasing as the region being searched becomes smaller. For a frame to be declared voiced, the peak must be greater than $0.4R(0)$, where $R(0)$ is the value of the autocorrelation function at zero time-lag; otherwise the frame is declared unvoiced.

4.6.4 Post-processing of pitch contours

Most good pitch detection algorithms have a post-processing or error-correction module in their final stage. This corrects for any obvious errors in the pitch estimates and provides some form of smoothing of the pitch contour. A check is made to ensure that an unvoiced frame cannot occur between two voiced frames. If this situation is detected, the offending frame is re-designated as voiced and is assigned a pitch value to the average of the two surrounding frames. Finally, to correct for pitch estimation errors, the pitch contours are smoothed. This can be achieved by simple low-pass filtering but often a special type of filter known as a *median of N* filter is used. A median of N filter operates on N input samples $x[n]$, $x[n-1], \ldots, x[n-N+1]$, places them in ascending order of amplitude and selects the median (middle) sample as the filter output. For smoothing pitch contours, filter lengths N of 3 and 5 have been found useful for correcting occasional errors.

4.7 Phonetic analysis

The aim in phonetic analysis is to derive the phonemic structure of an utterance directly from the speech signal. The sequence of phonemes correspond to a sequence of articulatory gestures, which have certain, well-defined acoustic equivalents. However, as discussed in chapter 1, the acoustic–phonetic mapping is exceedingly complex. There is no simple one-to-one relationship between a phoneme and its acoustic equivalents. Co-articulation effects cause overlap between phonemic boundaries and the acoustic correlates of a phoneme are modified by its neighbours (allophonic variation). In addition, speakers can sometimes distort the acoustic characteristics of speech sounds to such an extent that they no longer possess the characteristics normally associated with their class. For example, the vowel /e/ in the word destroy can become unvoiced, so that it no longer resembles a vowel. The task of phonetic analysis is therefore an extremely difficult one and great care has to be taken when designing a suitable algorithm.

The most popular way to perform a phonetic analysis is to attempt to segment the speech signal into phonemic-like units and to assign an appropriate label to each unit. This process is generally known as *segmentation and labelling* and involves an analysis of the time-varying acoustic features of the speech signal. The features typically used include pitch, zero-crossing rate, energy profiles, spectral shape and formant frequencies and trajectories. The speech is normally analysed in 10–20 ms time-frames and the acoustic features are extracted. The next step is to segment the signal into phonemic-size units. This involves examining the acoustic feature set and placing boundaries where values exceed pre-determined thresholds. The features that are typically used include energy profiles, zero-crossing rate and spectral rate of change. In more sophisticated systems, the apparent phonetic context is used to determine exactly the features and thresholds to use, instead of using the same features for each boundary decision. For example, if a time region is thought to be one of the glides /w, r, l/ then the boundary between the glide and the adjacent vowel is best located by examining the formant frequency trajectories. This type of algorithm is therefore based on acoustic–phonetic knowledge which has to be formalised and stored as rules in the system. Unfortunately, at present, there are large gaps in this knowledge and much basic research is required to fill them.

Once the boundaries have been located, labels have to be assigned by each phonemic unit. This is normally carried out by comparing the features of the unit to be labelled with a set of prototypical features for each phoneme, which are stored in the system. For speaker-independent analysis, these prototypical features should be based on data from a wide variety of speakers. Individual vowels can normally be identified by the steady-state values of the first three formant frequency values extracted from the centre of the vowel. Diphthongs are characterised by the values of the formant frequencies in the initial and final vowel targets, as well as the rate of change of the formant trajectories. Nasals and glides always occur adjacent to a vowel and can be characterised by the formant transitions into and out of the sound. Fricatives can be detected through the presence or absence of turbulent noise and can often be identified by their gross spectral shape. Plosives are characterised by a period of silence followed by an abrupt increase in signal level at the point of release, followed by a burst of frication noise. Plosive types can be identified by measurements which include the frequency spectrum of the burst, the formant transitions in adjacent vowels and voice on-set time (the time between the energy release and the onset of voicing in the following vowel).

Unfortunately, phonetic analysis using segmentation and labelling is extremely error-prone. Certain segments may be incorrectly identified, more than one phoneme may be grouped together in a single segment and also a single phoneme may be sometimes split into more than one segment. One way of accounting for the possibility of errors is to present the output of the phonetic analyser in the form of a *phonetic lattice*. This is used in a number of systems and involves listing a number of candidate phonemes for each time-unit together with a confidence measure for each phoneme. The ambiguities are then resolved by higher levels of linguistic processing, which normally involves matching the possible phonemic sequences against entries in the system lexicon, in order to postulate possible utterances and select the most likely.

Not all phonetic analysers operate on the principle of segmentation and labelling. Another approach is to propose sequences of phonemes, use a speech synthesis by rule algorithm (section 5.6) to generate the acoustic templates, and then compare these with the input templates. Alternative sequences can be evaluated and one that provides the closest match is selected as the phonemic structure of the input speech.

Phonetic analysis is still a major problem in speech analysis and is still probably one of the greatest obstacles to the development of powerful speech recognition systems (chapter 7), as well as very low bit-rate speech coding systems (chapter 6). Much research is required to determine the precise nature of the complex acoustic–phonetic transformation.

5 Speech Synthesis

Speech synthesis is the process of producing an acoustic signal by controlling a model of speech production with a set of parameters. If the model and parameters are sufficiently accurate then the production of intelligible synthetic speech should be possible. There are two basic approaches in modelling the speech production process. One is a direct approach which attempts to model the system in detail. This is commonly referred to as *articulatory speech synthesis* and attempts to directly model the motion of the speech articulators as well as the generation and propagation of sound inside the vocal tract. This approach is still the subject of research and although it seems to have the potential for producing the most natural-sounding speech in the long term, it has not as yet been as successful as approaches that attempt to simply copy the frequency response characteristic of the vocal tract. Such approaches are based on the source/filter model developed in chapter 1 and are collectively known as *terminal–analogue synthesisers* since they use a system which is an analogue of the speech production mechanism from a terminal point of view.

This chapter considers the construction and operation of the most popular types of terminal–analogue speech synthesiser. A brief discussion of articulatory speech synthesis is also given.

5.1 History of speech synthesis

One of the earliest documented attempts at speech synthesis was made in 1779 when a Russian scientist called Kratzenstein constructed a set of five acoustic resonators (figure 5.1) which, when activated by a vibrating reed, produced imitations of the vowels. In 1791 Wolfgang Von Kemplen, a Hungarian, constructed a more elaborate machine which could be made to speak whole words and phrases. As illustrated in figure 5.2, it consisted of a large bellows which supplied a stream of air to a reed which, in turn, excited a hand-held rubber tube (resonator). Extra tubes and whistles were added to imitate the nasal and fricative sounds. A much more recent mechanical speech synthesiser was constructed by Reisz in 1937. The motion of the speech articulators was simulated by pressing keys to vary the shape of mechanical vocal tract. It could produce connected speech when operated by a skilled person.

Figure 5.1   Kratzenstein's acoustic resonators

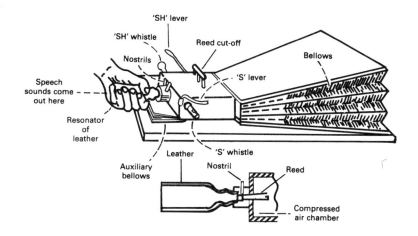

Figure 5.2   Von Kempelen's talking machine

The development of electronics signalled the demise of mechanical synthesisers and heralded the production of more successful electrical ones. One of the first was a device called the Voder (figure 5.3), built in 1938. This attempted to model the vocal tract electrically using ten contiguous bandpass filters, connected in parallel, which spanned the speech frequency band and were excited by a periodic buzz source or a random-noise source. The gains of the bandpass filters, the choice of buzz or noise excitation and the pitch of the buzz source could be controlled by finger keys, a wrist-bar and a foot-pedal respectively. After considerable practice, it was possible to manipulate the Voder to produce intelligible speech.

The desire to reduce the transmission bandwidth of speech in telephony led to Dudley's invention of the Vocoder in 1939. As shown in figure 5.4, the Vocoder consists of both an analyser and a synthesiser. The analyser consists of a set of ten bandpass filters, connected in parallel, covering the speech frequency band. The amplitude of the filter outputs, a voiced/unvoiced decision and the pitch frequency for voiced speech are continuously measured, multiplexed and transmitted to the synthesiser. At the synthesiser end, the parameters are demultiplexed and used to control the

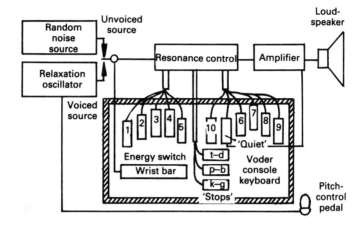

Figure 5.3   The Voder electronic synthesiser

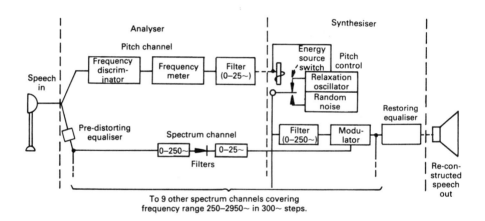

Figure 5.4   Block diagram of Vocoder

gains of a set of bandpass filters, identical to those used in the analyser.
These filters are excited by either a pulse source, whose frequency is
controlled by the pitch parameter, or a noise source, selected by the
voiced/unvoiced parameter. The speech signal is reconstructed by summing the outputs of the bandpass filters. Because of the relatively slow-
varying properties of the pitch and the speech spectrum compared with the
speech signal itself, the parameters which define these quantities can be
transmitted using about one-tenth of the bandwidth required by the speech
signal.

In contrast to the aforementioned electrical methods which synthesised speech by attempting to model the speech signal itself, the Electrical Vocal Tract designed by Dunn in the late 1940s attempted to model the detail of speech production. He represented the vocal tract as an acoustic transmission line by splitting it into a series of cylindrical sections (figure 5.5(a)) and then showed how each could be represented by an equivalent electrical network, with the values of the elements in the network being derived from the dimensions and physical properties of the vocal tract. He built a transmission-line model which consisted of 25 inductor–capacitor T-networks each representing a cylinder 0.5 cm long and 6 cm² in cross-section (figure 5.5(b)). The line could be divided into two sections, representing two cavities, by inserting a variable inductance between any two sections of the line to represent the tongue-hump constriction. Another variable inductance at the end of the line represented the lip termination. A high-impedance waveform generator was applied to the input of the line to produce vowel sounds.

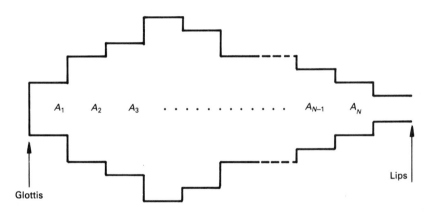

(a) Cylindrical acoustic-tube representation

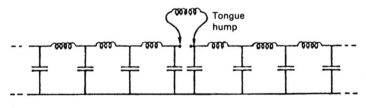

(b) Equivalent transmission line model

Figure 5.5   Dunn's electrical vocal-tract model

In 1953, a time-domain approach to the speech synthesis problem was pioneered by Lawrence who utilised the fact that the response of resonant systems, like the resonant cavities of the vocal tract, to impulsive excitation is a damped sinusoidal oscillation. The frequency of the oscillation is dependent on the resonant frequency of the system and the damping factor on the bandwidth of the system. Lawrence produced voiced sounds by adding together three damped sinusoids. The damping function for each pitch period was produced by a fixed decaying exponential signal which was effectively multiplied by three individual sinusoids. The frequencies of these sinusoids were inferred from spectrogram measurements.

All of the early speech synthesisers, both articulatory and terminal–analogue types, were constructed using analogue circuits. These devices were difficult to control and proper evaluation of their capacity for producing good-quality speech could not be carried out. The developments in digital computing in the 1960s greatly revolutionised speech research. It then became possible not only to simulate new synthesiser designs but also to use digital computers to supply data to control the synthesiser in order to carry out a proper evaluation.

For the interested reader, a comprehensive history of speech synthesis may be found in the book by Linggard (1985).

5.2 Formant synthesisers

Formant synthesisers are of the terminal–analogue type. They are generally implemented using electrical networks, either analogue or digital, having frequency response characteristics similar to that of the vocal tract. These networks are excited by an electrical source similar to the sound source exciting the vocal tract, that is a quasi-periodic pulse generator in the case of voiced sounds and a random-noise generator for unvoiced sounds. Figure 5.6 shows suitable circuits for these two sources which work reasonably well, though for complete naturalness the output of the pulse source should closely match natural glottal pulses. The voiced sound source in figure 5.6(a) is derived by integrating the square-wave output of a hysterisis comparator to produce a triangular-wave source. Frequency control of the output can be achieved by varying resistor R_4 electronically. The potentiometer R_8 may be use to vary the mark–space ratio of the comparator output and hence the shape of the triangular-wave output. The unvoiced source in figure 5.6(b) is obtained by amplifying the white noise produced when the base–emitter junction of a transistor is sufficiently reverse-biased for breakdown to occur. In a digital formant synthesiser, random noise is obtained by generating a pseudo-random sequence of numbers, with a random number being generated at each sampling instant.

Each vocal tract resonance or formant is simulated by a second-order

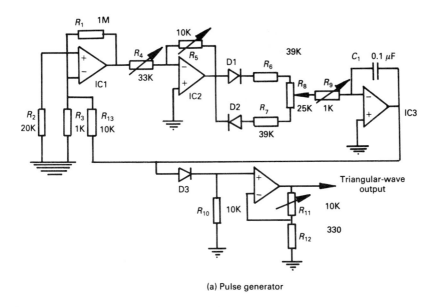

(a) Pulse generator

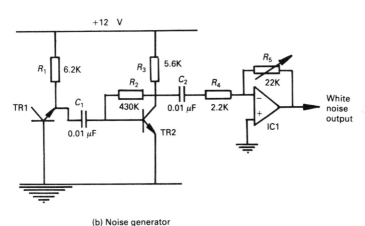

(b) Noise generator

Figure 5.6 Synthesiser sound sources

resonant circuit with variable centre frequency and perhaps bandwidth. The typical frequency ranges of the first three formants of speech, F_1, F_2 and F_3, are as follows: F_1 – 100 Hz to 1000 Hz; F_2 – 700 Hz to 2500 Hz; and F_3 – 1500 Hz to 3500 Hz. The bandwidth of each formant also varies though, compared with formant frequency, this is perceptually less significant and formant bandwidths are often kept fixed in a synthesiser. It has been shown that the minimum percentage change in formant frequency

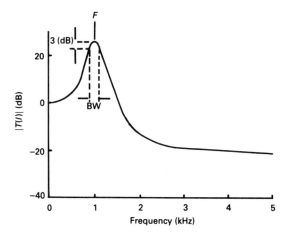

Figure 5.7   Typical frequency response of formant resonator

that can be detected by the human ear is about 5 per cent. The correspond-ing figure for formant bandwidth is about 40 per cent.

The frequency response of a typical second-order resonator is shown in figure 5.7. In the synthesiser a number of these responses are combined to produce maxima in the overall frequency response of the synthesiser corresponding to the formants of the vocal tract. At least three formant resonators are normally used but very often a fourth is used to improve voice quality.

The s-domain transfer function, $H(s)$, of a second-order resonator is given by

$$H(s) \;=\; \frac{\omega_0^2}{s^2 + bs + \omega_0^2} \tag{5.1}$$

where ω_0 and b are the radian centre frequency and bandwidth respectively of the circuit. The circuit diagram of an analogue formant resonator, realised using a biquadratic operational amplifier circuit, is shown in figure 5.8(a). An analysis of the circuit shows that its transfer function has the general form of equation (5.1) where $\omega_0 = \{R_2/(R_3C_1C_2)\}^{1/2}$. R, $b = 1/C_1R_4$, $K = \{(R_2R_4)/(R_1R_3)\}$. It is possible to vary the resonant frequency ω_0 linearly without affecting the bandwidth b or the gain K by keeping R_2, R_3, C_1 and C_2 fixed, making $R_5 = R_6 = R$ and varying them electronically. Many of the most popular techniques for achieving this are discussed by Linggard (1985).

Alternatively each resonator may be implemented with a digital filter with transfer function

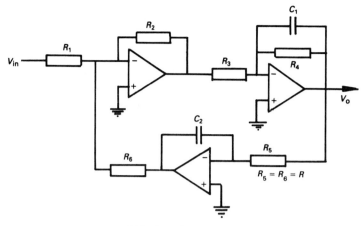

(a) Analogue formant resonator

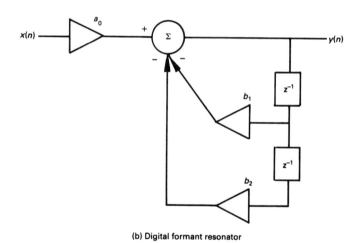

(b) Digital formant resonator

Figure 5.8   Formant resonators

$$H(z) = a_0/(1 + b_1 z^{-1} + b_2 z^{-2}) \tag{5.2}$$

where $a_0 \quad = 1 - 2e^{-bT/2} \cdot \cos\{(\omega_0^2 - b^2/4)^{1/2} \cdot T\} + e^{-bT}$,

$b_1 \quad = -2e^{bT/2} \cdot \cos\{(\omega_0^2 - b^2/4)^{1/2} \cdot T\}$,

$b_2 \quad = e^{-bT}$,

$T \quad =$ sample period.

Signal Processing of Speech

Figure 5.8(b) shows the filter realisation. The expressions for the digital filter coefficients, a_0, b_1 and b_2, are obtained by transforming the s-domain transfer function of equation (5.1) using the method of impulse invariance. In the impulse invariant method of filter design, the impulse (unit-sample) response of the digital filter is made identical to the sampled impulse response of the prototype analogue filter (see problems 5.1 and 5.2).

The formant generators may be connected either in series or in parallel to give a serial synthesiser or a parallel synthesiser respectively. In a serial synthesiser, the output of one formant resonator provides the input to the next as shown in figure 5.9.

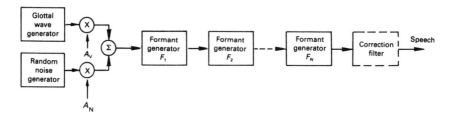

Figure 5.9   Basic serial formant synthesiser

Normally three formant filters would be used with the effects of the higher-frequency formants being lumped together in a single higher-formant correction filter. This is essentially a spectral-flattening filter which compensates for the cumulative attenuation of the -12 dB/octave roll-off of each formant filter at the higher frequencies. The correction filter is shown dotted because it is only required in analogue implementations. It is not necessary in digital implementations because of the different nature of the digital resonator frequency response above resonance. It rolls off at a lesser rate at higher frequencies and is in fact flat at half the sampling frequency. It has been shown that digital synthesisers without any higher-formant correction give a closer approximation to the vocal tract response than analogue synthesisers with higher-formant correction.

The serial structure shown in figure 5.9 can give a very close approximation to the vocal tract response for non-nasalised vowel and vowel-like sounds. In addition, formant amplitudes are a function of all the formant frequencies and bandwidths and do not have to be explicitly controlled. However, as it stands, it is incapable of accurately simulating the anti-resonances or zeros which occur in the production of nasals, fricatives and stops. There are many approaches which can be adopted for producing these types of sounds in a serial formant synthesiser. For the production of nasals, a pole–zero network may be added in series with the resonators of figure 5.9. Alternatively, this network, or perhaps a single resonator, may

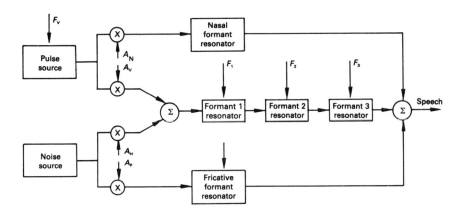

Figure 5.10   Complete serial formant synthesiser

be added in parallel. An additional pole–zero filter is often added in parallel to produce stops and fricatives.

A block diagram of a complete serial formant synthesiser is shown in figure 5.10. It consists of three low-pass resonators with variable centre frequency (F_1, F_2, F_3), connected in series, and separate parallel filters for producing nasals and fricatives. The resonant frequency of the nasal formant is held fixed while the resonant frequency of the fricative filter is variable (F_F). There are four amplitude control parameters; A_V and A_N are voicing amplitudes for the oral and nasal tracts respectively while A_H and A_F are aspiration and frication amplitudes. The pitch of the voiced excitation is controlled by F_V.

In a parallel-formant synthesiser the formant generators are connected in parallel and their outputs are weighted and summed to produce the synthetic speech signal as shown in figure 5.11. Note that the formant amplitudes are specified as well as the formant frequencies. This gives more parameters to control but is advantageous in that it allows greater control over the shape of the frequency spectrum of the synthesised speech. In the design of parallel-formant synthesisers, a low-pass, second-order resonator is normally used for formant 1 and second-order bandpass resonators for the higher formants. It is easily shown that the transfer function of a parallel connection of resonators contains zeros as well as poles. This is advantageous for producing nasals and fricatives but can lead to deep minima between the formant peaks for vowel and vowel-like sounds. These minima can be eliminated by alternating the signs of the formant amplitudes and this is normally done in parallel-formant synthesiser design. Additional circuits are often added in parallel with the basic structure of figure 5.11 to assist in the production of nasals, fricatives and stops.

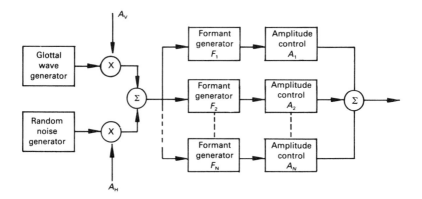

Figure 5.11   Basic parallel formant synthesiser

Perhaps the most well-known parallel formant synthesiser is the JSRU (Joint Speech Research Unit) synthesiser shown in figure 5.12 [Holmes, 1985]. It uses three variable-frequency formant resonators to simulate the first three formants of the vocal tract and a fixed-frequency (3500 Hz) fourth formant resonator. At the outputs of the resonators are spectral-shaping or correction filters which ensure that the combined filter response rolls off at the correct rate above the resonant frequencies. Nasal and fricative circuits are added in parallel with the basic structure. There are five amplitude controls, one for each of the four formants and the nasal formant. The fundamental frequency of the glottal waveform generator is variable as is its pulse width. There is a mechanism for varying formant bandwidths in the JSRU synthesiser though this is internal to' the synthesiser and the bandwidths are not explicitly controlled.

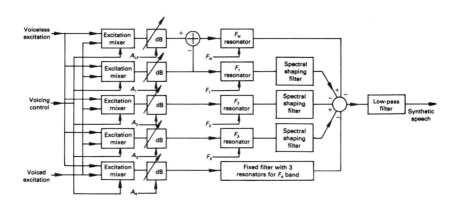

Figure 5.12   JSRU parallel formant synthesiser

A serial synthesiser is a better model of the vocal tract for the production of vowel and vowel-like sounds whereas a parallel synthesiser is better suited to producing nasals, fricatives and stops. In order to exploit the best features of both types of synthesiser, a combined serial/parallel-formant synthesiser known as the Klatt synthesiser has been developed by the eminent speech researcher Denis Klatt [Klatt, 1980]. A block diagram of this synthesiser is shown in figure 5.13. It uses a series connection of resonators to produce non-nasal voiced sounds and a parallel connection to produce nasals, fricatives and stops. Parameters denoted by the symbol A are amplitude controls while blocks labelled with the symbol R denote resonators with variable frequency and bandwidth. RNP is a nasal resonator and RNZ is a nasal anti-resonator, both with variable frequency and bandwidth. RGP, RGZ and RGS are glottal spectral-shaping filters which can be used to model more accurately the voicing characteristics of a given speaker.

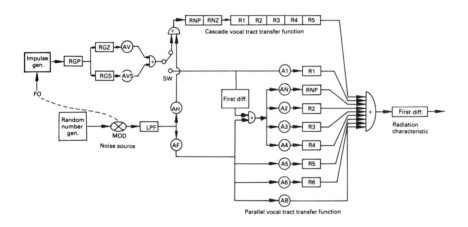

Figure 5.13   Klatt synthesiser

In order to produce connected speech from a formant synthesiser, a set of control parameters are supplied to the synthesiser every 10–20 ms. If these parameters are sufficiently accurate then good-quality synthetic speech can result. In fact, if properly controlled, many formant synthesisers are capable of producing speech which is virtually indistinguishable from the natural speech from which the synthesiser control parameters were derived. However this can take a lot of time and effort, and can require a great deal of manual fine-tuning of the parameter values. Developing a system that automatically copies human utterances using a formant synthesiser is a difficult problem.

5.3 Linear predictive synthesisers

The technique of linear prediction was described in section 4.8 and it was shown there that if the error signal and the linear predictor coefficients $\{a_i, i = 1, 2, \ldots, p\}$ are known then the original speech signal can be reconstructed by applying the error signal to an all-pole digital filter with transfer function

$$H(z) = 1 \left/ \left(1 - \sum_{k=1}^{p} a_k z^{-k}\right)\right. \tag{5.3}$$

When viewed in this way, it is clear that the process of linear prediction results in a source–filter model of speech production in which the error signal represents the excitation signal and the vocal tract is represented by the all-pole filter $H(z)$. This leads to the structure of a linear predictive synthesiser (figure 5.14) in which the error signal is 'stylised' as a periodic unit sample generator at pitch frequency in the case of voiced speech or a random-number generator in the case of unvoiced speech. The synthetic speech samples are given by the equation

$$\tilde{x}[n] = \sum_{k=1}^{p} (a_k \cdot x[n - k]) + G \cdot u[n] \tag{5.4}$$

where $u[n]$ is a unit-step sequence and G is a gain control parameter which determines the r.m.s. value of the synthesised signal. In order to synthesise connected speech using this synthesiser, a time-varying set of control parameters are required which specify the pitch-period, a voiced/unvoiced decision, the gain G and the p predictor coefficients. These parameters would be typically supplied every 10–20 ms though, for voiced sounds, they

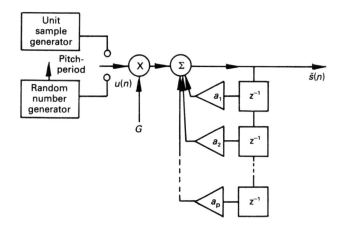

Figure 5.14   Linear predictive synthesiser

would normally be constrained to change pitch synchronously, that is at the beginning of each glottal cycle. This is much preferable to a pitch-asynchronous update in that the coefficients are changed when the filter contains minimum energy and this reduces the effect of the sensitivity of the filter structure to coefficient change. However, the pitch-synchronous method requires that the control parameters be interpolated to obtain the values at the beginning of each pitch period.

One problem with the synthesis structure shown in figure 5.14 is that an unstable filter may result if the a_k coefficients are quantised using a small number of bits or if they are interpolated to provide a pitch-synchronous update. This can be overcome by deriving an alternative synthesis structure which uses a different set of coefficients called reflection coefficients. These can be derived from the a_k coefficients using a step-down recursion procedure. Although we will not consider the theoretical details here, reflection coefficients always lie in the range ±1 for stable filters and are much less sensitive to quantisation effects than the predictor coefficients themselves. Synthetic speech is generated from the predictor coefficients in a structure known as a lattice filter which is illustrated in figure 5.15. There are p stages in the lattice where p is the order of the linear predictor. The error signal, either real or stylised, is input at the top left-hand corner of the lattice and is modified as it passes along the top towards the right-hand end where the speech signal emerges. The signal is fed back along the bottom path through a series of delays, the outputs of which are used to modify the forward-travelling signal at various points in the path. The backward-travelling signal eventually passes out through the bottom left-hand corner of the lattice and is discarded.

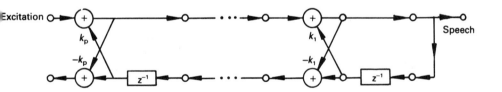

Figure 5.15   Lattice filter synthesiser

5.4 Copy synthesis

In the previous sections, it has been indicated that intelligible speech may be generated if a speech synthesiser, either formant or LPC-based, is controlled by an appropriate, time-varying set of parameters which are specified at typically 10–20 ms time-intervals. The design and construction of a suitable synthesiser is however only a small part of the task of generating synthetic speech; a significant problem is how to obtain a set of control parameters to produce a particular utterance. One of the most obvious ways of doing this is to derive the control parameters from an analysis of real speech. In the case of linear prediction, the analysis process is completely automatic (section 3.7) and, provided that the prediction error signal is adequately reproduced, the resulting re-synthesised speech can be of very high quality and virtually indistinguishable from the original. The same is true of formant-based synthesisers, except that error-free automation of the formant extraction process (section 4.5) is virtually impossible to achieve and some manual intervention and 'massaging' of the formant frequency contours is required.

The technique of producing synthetic speech by analysing real speech is often referred to as 'speech analysis/synthesis' or simply 'copy synthesis'. The main application area for this technique is in information services, in which only a small vocabulary of words or a fixed set of messages is required. In such systems, the speech signal is encoded in the synthesiser control parameters and stored either in semiconductor memory or on a magnetic medium (such as a floppy disk). The advantage of this technique over direct storage of the original time-domain speech signal is one of economy of storage. Speech sampled at 8 kHz and quantised to 8 bits/sample (for example, 8-bit log PCM) corresponds to a data rate of 64 kbits/s. Therefore, for direct speech the storage capacity per 8 kbytes of semiconductor memory is approximately 1 second $\{(8 \times 1024 \times 8)/64\,000\}$ and per 1 Mbyte of disk storage 131 s $\{(1024 \times 1024 \times 8)/64\,000\}$. Contrast these storage capacities with a case of formant-encoded speech which consists of 8×6-bit parameters specified every 20 ms (50 frames/s). The data rate in this case is $8 \times 6 \times 50 = 2400$ bits/s. The corresponding storage capacity figures are 27 seconds $\{(8 \times 1024 \times 8)/2400\}$ per 8 kbytes of semiconductor memory and 58 minutes $\{(1024 \times 1024 \times 8)/2400\}$ per 1 Mbyte of disk storage. These figures represent a compression by a factor of approximately 27. A similar compression is possible in the case of *LPC*-encoded speech.

The main problem with copy synthesis is that it cannot be used where a large or unlimited vocabulary is required and where a wide variety of messages has to be generated. A speech recording and analysis session is also required.

5.5 Phoneme synthesis

Another way of obtaining synthesiser control parameters is to generate them from a phonetic transcription of the utterance. In other words, the utterance to be synthesised, represented by a string of phonemes, is input to a computer program, which outputs the sequence of synthesiser control parameters. The computer program is generally based on rules for converting phonetic information to acoustic information; for this reason, the synthesis process is often referred to as *speech synthesis by rule*. The system must also have some method of assigning prosodic information (intonation and stress) to the utterance, otherwise it will sound completely unnatural. This is normally achieved by inserting prosodic markers or symbols in the input phonemic string and will be described in more detail later.

It was indicated in sections 1.4 and 1.5 that although speech may be viewed simply as a sequence of segmental units (phonemes) at a linguistic level, the manifestation of these units at the acoustic level is much more complex. The mechanism of co-articulation, which results in sounds being smeared together, is one of the major influences on speech naturalness. Co-articulation results in complex movements of the formant frequency and amplitude values between one sound and the next. There are also many acoustic variations of each phoneme (allophones), depending on its context (place) in an utterance. The synthesis by rule program must simulate these effects as closely as possible, if it is to be successful in producing natural-sounding synthetic speech. A speech synthesis-by-rule system therefore normally contains at least the following four components:

(i) a 'look-up table' storing target or steady-state formant frequency and amplitude values;

(ii) data and rules for generating formant transitions between neighbouring sounds;

(iii) data the rules for allowing allophonic variation of sounds depending on the nature of the surrounding speech;

(iv) a mechanism for assigning a prosodic pattern to the utterance.

The look-up table from a relatively simple, yet very effective, synthesis-by-rule system developed by Ainsworth (1974) is given in table 5.1. This table consists of a steady-state formant frequency and amplitude values of the first three formants $\{F_1, A_1, F_2, A_2, F_3, A_3\}$ for each phoneme. The amplitude of a fixed-frequency (3500 Hz) fourth formant (A_4) is also specified. The SW parameter is either 0 or 1, depending on whether the corresponding phoneme is voiced or unvoiced respectively. T_1 and T_2 are duration parameters (ms) which respectively determine the steady duration of each phoneme and the transition time between that phoneme and the next. The method of calculating the formant frequency and amplitude parameters is given in figure 5.16, which illustrates the calculation of the F_2 trajectory at 10 ms time-intervals for the word sit $\{/s\text{ɪ}t/\}$. In the phoneme /s/, F_2 has a steady-state value of 1720 Hz and lasts for 100 ms (10 × 10 ms frames). The transition time between the steady-state /s/ values and the next sound is 20 ms. Therefore the F_2 value must reach the /ɪ/ steady-state value of 2080 Hz in this time. Since linear transitions are assumed, one

Signal Processing of Speech

Table 5.1   Phoneme look-up table, after Ainsworth (1974)

Phoneme	F_1 SW(Hz)	A_1 (dB)	F_2 (Hz)	A_2 (dB)	F_3 (Hz)	A_3 (dB)	A_4 (dB)	T_1 (ms)	T_2 (ms)
/b/	1 220	35	760	28	2500	28	28	10	30
/d/	1 220	28	1780	28	2620	28	35	20	30
/g/	1 220	28	1960	35	2620	28	28	20	30
/p/	1 220	28	760	28	2500	28	0	50	30
/t/	1 220	28	1780	28	2620	28	40	50	30
/k/	1 220	28	1960	40	2620	28	28	50	30
/m/	0 220	35	1000	19	2200	26	0	60	10
/n/	0 220	45	1300	19	2620	26	16	60	10
/ŋ/	0 310	51	820	33	2800	28	26	60	10
/w/	0 220	35	760	28	1960	21	14	20	80
/r/	0 490	35	1120	28	1600	21	14	20	80
/l/	0 460	35	1480	28	2500	21	14	20	80
/ʃ/	0 220	35	2500	28	2980	21	14	20	80
/n/	1 580	0	1660	28	2440	28	0	60	60
/f/	1 400	0	1420	23	2740	37	35	60	60
/θ/	1 400	0	1780	26	2440	28	23	60	60
/s/	1 400	0	1720	28	2440	28	40	100	20
/j/	1 400	0	2020	31	2920	42	31	100	20
/v/	1 280	30	1420	40	2740	37	33	40	40
/ð/	1 280	30	1600	31	2380	26	28	40	40
/z/	1 280	30	1720	24	2320	24	38	40	40
/ʒ/	1 280	30	2020	26	2740	37	26	40	40
/i/	0 250	51	2320	33	2740	37	31	60	50
/I/	0 400	51	2080	37	2680	35	30	30	30
/ɛ/	0 640	51	2020	42	2800	38	31	40	40
/æ/	0 790	41	1780	47	2800	38	31	50	50
/a/	0 790	51	1060	49	2500	30	23	80	80
/ə/	0 610	51	880	48	2260	23	16	50	40
/ɔ/	0 490	51	820	45	2500	30	17	80	80
/u/	0 340	51	1000	42	2440	28	23	30	30
/u/	0 250	51	880	38	2080	17	10	70	70
/ʌ/	0 700	51	1360	44	2560	31	24	50	40
/ɜ/	0 580	51	1420	45	2620	33	26	80	80
/ə/	0 490	51	1480	51	2620	33	26	40	40

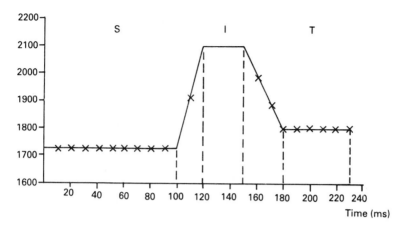

Figure 5.16   Example of formant (F_2) trajectory calculation in phoneme synthesis

intermediate F_2 value of 1900 Hz at $t = 110$ ms can be calculated as shown. The steady-state duration of /ɪ/ is 30 ms and this gives rise to a constant F_2 value of 2080 Hz for three consecutive frames up to a time $t = 150$ ms. The process then continues in a similar fashion to compute the /ɪ/ – /t/ transition and the steady-state part of /t/. The process is identical for the other formant frequency and amplitude parameters, and can therefore be used to generate a sequence of control parameters, specified at 10 ms time-intervals for a parallel-formant speech synthesiser.

Unfortunately, the simple parameter generation procedure outlined above is incapable, on its own, of producing high-quality synthetic speech; there are numerous exceptions and additional small details which have to be taken into account. For example, the steady-state part of the plosive sounds /b, d, g, p, t, k/ is actually silence and what distinguishes one from another are the formant transitions just before and after the silent steady-state part and the burst of aspiration which occurs at the end of the phoneme. An improvement in naturalness can be obtained by storing allophones of certain phonemes, which are known to vary widely in different contexts. Linear formant transitions are not very realistic and many synthesis systems use non-linear formant trajectories which are modelled as the output of first-order or critically damped second-order systems with time-constants which may be different for each formant or which may vary depending on the phoneme.

Even if co-articulation effects and allophonic variations are modelled very well, the synthetic speech will not sound natural, unless an adequate mechanism exists for superimposing prosodic information on the utterance. This normally involves assigning the following three components:

(i)   an appropriate pitch or intonation contour;
(ii) phoneme duration which largely comprises lengthening the vowels to
      be stressed in the utterance;
(iii) pause-insertion.

A variety of methods has been developed for assigning prosodic patterns to a phonemic input string. In the earliest techniques, pitch and duration values for every phoneme in the input string were individually specified. This was clearly a difficult and cumbersome task. Most prosodic algorithms now use some form of notation in which numbers, markers and delimiters in the input phonemic string indicate the pitch contour, the stressed syllables and the overall rhythm (including pauses) of the utterance. A typical example of this notation from Witten (1982) for the utterance 'automatic synthesis of speech from a phonetic representation' is as follows:

3ˆaw t uh/ m aa tik/ sinth uh sis uhv/ * speetsh 1ˆ fruhm uh fuh/*
netik/ repruhzen/ teish uhn.

The standard IPA phonetic symbols are coded into one or two letters to suit conventional computer keyboards. Phoneme duration is calculated in accordance with the *isochronous foot* theory of speech rhythm. The word 'foot' in this context refers to the time-interval between successive stressed syllables and the isochronous theory states that the duration of each syllable in a foot is adjusted to make the duration of each foot approximately constant (*isochronous* = 'of equal time'). In the example above, the foot stress is indicated by a '/' occurring after the syllable. A '*' occurring before a syllable indicates a point of tonic stress (maximum pitch value of an intonation contour). All other syllables are unstressed. The utterance is divided by punctuation marks into tone groups (two in the above example) and the shape of the intonation contour is specified by a number at the start of each one, that is 3 and 1 above. Pause insertion is achieved through the use of full-stops. The 'ˆ'character denotes a breath-point.

Speech synthesis from a phonemic input provides a convenient and extremely economical representation of speech utterances for storage. Forty or fifty phonemes plus a few prosodic markers can be encoded using 6 bits and, with a normal speaking rate of about 12 phonemes per second, the data rate is $6 \times 12 = 72$ bits/s. Thus 8 kilobytes of memory can store approximately 15 minutes of speech $\{(8192 \times 8)/72$ seconds$\}$ and 1 Mbyte of disk storage approximately 32 hours $\{(1024 \times 1024 \times 8)/72$ seconds$\}$.

Apart from the phenomenal storage efficiency, another major advantage of phonemic synthesis over copy synthesis is that, given adequate hardware and software, utterances in the form of phonetic text can be stored as the arguments of a 'SPEAK' command and output to the speech synthesiser at appropriate instances during the execution of a computer program. Also new utterances can be generated immediately without the need for a recording and analysis session. One inconvenience is that application programmers must acquire a skill in phonetic transcription.

5.6 Concatenation of multi-phonemic units

In order to circumvent the difficult problem of writing rules to simulate co-articulation in phonemic synthesis, one approach has been to use larger phonetic units, such as diphones, syllables or even words, which inherently possess the strong inter-phoneme co-articulation effects. Sufficient samples of each of the relevant units are acquired, analysed and a parametric representation is stored in the system (formants, LPC coefficients etc.). Speech is synthesised by concatenating these in sequence using fairly simple rules to interpolate the parameter values at the unit boundaries. Of course, in all of these systems, a mechanism for assigning an appropriate prosodic pattern to the overall utterance is still required. For this reason, the pitch and timing of the original unit is discarded.

Diphones are units which span two sounds – from the centre of one phone to the centre of the next. The acoustic features are relatively invariant in the middle of a phone and the co-articulation effects are captured in the transition between the two phones. It has been determined that at least 1000 diphones are required to synthesise speech of a reasonable quality. However, for high-quality synthesis, a far greater number of diphones are required.

Other larger units which might be suitable for concatenation are the syllable and demi-syllable. A syllable consists of an initial consonant cluster $\{C_i\}$, followed by a vowel or diphthong $\{V\}$ and then a final consonant cluster $\{C_f\}$, that is C_iVC_f. The syllable is not very suitable for concatenation, since strong co-articulation effects between adjacent syllables would have to be modelled. Also, the number of syllables is prohibitively large; it has been estimated that there are about 10 000 syllables in the English language. A more suitable unit is the demi-syllable, which can be either an initial demi-syllable, defined from the beginning of the syllable to the middle of the vowel $\{C_iV\}$ or a final demi-syllable, defined from the middle of the vowel to the end of the syllable $\{VC_f\}$. There are about 2000 demi-syllables in English, 800 initial demi-syllables and 1200 final demi-syllables. Interpolation of the parameter values at demi-syllable boundaries is relatively straightforward, since co-articulation in these regions is weak.

The largest multi-phonemic unit used in concatenation systems is the word. It is a particularly attractive unit, since again all the co-articulation effects are stored within the word structure. Words can be easily strung together to form sentences, since the co-articulation between words is comparatively weak and no phonetic expertise is required. The main disadvantage of words, however, is that an exceedingly large vocabulary is required for unrestricted speech synthesis.

It is worth mentioning at this point that some word concatenation systems operate in the time domain; in other words, the time-waveform of each word is digitised and stored directly. The co-articulation effects within each word will be stored as before, as well as its prosodic features (pitch and rhythm). When such words are concatenated, the resulting speech is intelligible, though highly unnatural, since the pitch and rhythm of the sentence will be incorrect and it is impossible to correct it. Nevertheless, in applications where a small vocabulary is required and a limited dialogue takes place, such an approach can be successful and acceptable. Two examples of the use of this approach is British Telecom's speaking clock service over the telephone network and recorded messages concerning the change of telephone numbers. In this type of message, the multi-digit telephone number is formed by concatenating the time-waveforms (ADPCM – encoded) of digits recorded in isolation. The result is that the pitch and rhythm of the utterance sounds badly wrong on occasions but the message remains intelligible.

5.7 Text-to-speech synthesis

The basic goal in text-to-speech synthesis is to convert unrestricted text into natural-sounding speech. This requires two additional major tasks to those already described in phoneme synthesis. Firstly, the text must be translated into phonetics and secondly, the prosody of the speech must be determined directly from the textual representation. Unfortunately, these two tasks are not easily separated because stress and pronunciation are closely related. For example, the pronunciation of the adjectival and verbal forms of the word 'approximate' depends on which part of the word receives the stress. Another major influence on pronunciation and stress is semantics. For example, correct pronunciation/stress assignment for the word 'bow' in 'the archer's bow' and 'the ship's bow' depends on a semantic knowledge of the text. It is very difficult to incorporate this type of knowledge into a text-to-speech system.

In spite of these problems, a number of text-to-speech systems have been built, which can produce intelligible, though not natural-sounding, synthetic speech.

A block diagram showing the various stages in a typical text-to-speech system is shown in figure 5.17. The input to the system is unrestricted English text in the form of a sequence of printable characters, including

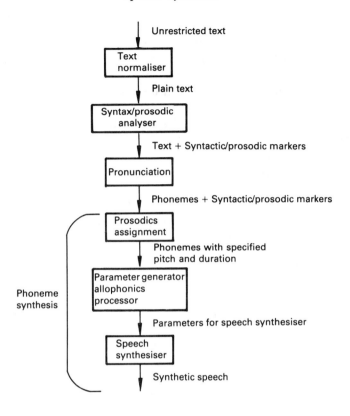

Figure 5.17   Block diagram of typical text-to-speech system

numbers, abbreviations and punctuation marks. The function of the text normaliser is to process any non-alphabetic characters: punctuation marks would be identified and left in place; abbreviations would be expanded to their full form; figures and monetary amounts would be expanded to their full form, for example '£2.75' would become 'two pounds and seventy-five pence'. The output of the text normaliser is plain text in the form of a sequence of alphabetic characters and punctuation marks.

The next module referred to in figure 5.17 as a Syntax/Prosodics Analyser uses some type of parsing algorithm to segment the text in such a way that meaningful intonation and rhythm can be assigned to it. This normally involves a grammatical analysis, that is the identification of noun phrases, verb phrases, prepositional phrases, conjunctions etc. The modules assign markers to the text which indicate, for example, the stressed syllables, the points of tonic stress of an intonation pattern and the types of intonation pattern to be used at various parts of the utterance.

The output of the Syntax/Prosodics Analyser, that is text plus syntax/

prosodics markers, is then input to the pronunciation module, which is required to compute the pronunciation of each word in the input text. The ultimate way of doing this would be to store every word in the language together with its phonetic equivalent, and pronunciation could then be effected using a simple dictionary look-up. However, the vast number of words in the language prohibit this approach because of the enormous size of the resulting dictionary. Practical systems tend to use pronunciation rules or letter-to-sound rules which specify the phonetic equivalent of single letters or groups of letters taking into account the context. This process is often assisted by the use of a small 'exceptions' dictionary which stores those words and their pronunciations which are constantly recurring and on which the letter-to-sound rules would fail. Thus an input is first checked against the entries in the dictionary and if it is not found, then the letter-to-sound rules are applied.

A very comprehensive system for English pronunciation has been developed by Allen [Allen *et al.*, 1987]. It consists of a *morph* dictionary, supplemented by letter-to-sound rules. A morph is either a prefix, a root or a suffix. Any word is either a root morph (for example, [view]), a root plus a prefix (for example, review = [re] + [view]), a root plus a suffix (for example, viewed = [view] + [ed]) or perhaps a compound root morph (for example, viewpoint = [view] + [point]). Estimates of the number of morph varies between 10 000 and 30 000. The number used by Allen in his system is about 10 000. The morph dictionary contains for each morph its spelling, pronunciation, part of speech etc. When a word is input to the system, a check is made to see if it exists in the dictionary. If not, it is input to an affix-stripping algorithm, which attempts to decompose the word into a prefix, a root and a suffix. If an affix can be stripped away, the reduced word is checked against the entries in the morph dictionary. If it still cannot be found, it is presented again to the affix-stripping algorithm. This process is repeated until the reduced word can be found in the morph dictionary or until the affix-stripping algorithm fails. If the morphic decomposition fails, the letter-to-sound rules are invoked in order to obtain the pronunciation.

The output of the pronunciation module is a sequence of phonemes together with syntactic/prosodic markers. The conversion of this representation into synthetic speech is carried out in a manner similar to that described for phonemic synthesis in section 5.5.

Text-to-speech has already been achieved on a commercial scale. At the time of writing (1991), it is possible to obtain, at reasonable cost, a number of systems, which can accept ordinary English text and convert it to speech which is highly intelligible, has reasonable rhythm and intonation qualities, but unfortunately, lacks any great naturalness. With some systems, it is possible to have a choice of voices, including male, female and children's voices. Some of these systems are based on phonemes, others on diphones.

Some use formant synthesisers as the output device, while others use an LPC synthesiser.

5.8 Articulatory speech synthesis

One of the greatest difficulties in the design of phoneme synthesis or text-to-speech synthesis is formulating a set of rules which can generate realistic formant transitions and accurately model co-articulation effects, which are essential for producing natural-sounding synthetic speech. Real speech is generated by a sequence of precisely-timed articulatory gestures and by trying to model this indirectly at the acoustic level, using segmental phonemic units, is perhaps too difficult a task. In the long term, it might prove easier to solve the naturalness problem by an approach to speech synthesis which models the detailed movements of the speech articulators as well as the generation and propagation of sound inside the vocal tract. This type of approach is generally referred to as *articulatory speech synthesis* and attempts to model the details of the speech production mechanism, instead of attempting to copy its frequency characteristics, as in conventional terminal-analogue synthesisers.

A block diagram showing the main components of a typical articulatory speech synthesiser is given in figure 5.18. It consists of three main components – an articulatory model, an acoustic-tube model and a vocal-cord model. The articulatory model transforms a set of perhaps 6–10 articulatory parameters, representing the position of the speech articulators (lips, tongue, jaw etc.) into a cross-sectional area function, $A(x)$, of the vocal tract. This function specifies the cross-sectional area of the tract at different positions, x, along its length and determines the 'shape' of an acoustic-tube model, which models the airflow and sound-wave propagation inside the vocal tract. The acoustic-tube is driven by an excitation model, which simulates the modulated airflow from the vocal cords and may include detailed modelling of cord vibration. Some account may also be taken of the effect of the vocal tract acoustic load on the vocal-cord output and the fact that the acoustics of the vocal tract are affected by the sub-glottal cavities. This is represented as 'interaction' between the cord and vocal-tract models in figure 5.18. Mechanisms for modelling turbulent airflow, for aspiration and frication are normally included within the acoustic-tube model.

If the system dynamics (parameter time-constants) are incorporated into the articulatory model, control of such a synthesiser is carried out by simply supplying a sequence of articulatory target parameters for the utterance to be synthesised. Co-articulation then takes place naturally without the need for complex rules. Also, the sounds produced by the

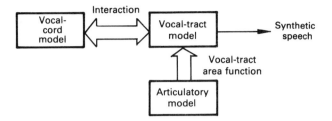

Figure 5.18 Block diagram of articulatory speech synthesiser

system must correspond to articulatory movements which are physically possible. Since the articulators move relatively slowly, the data rate for an articulatory synthesiser can theoretically be very low. It is thought that this may be as low as 50 bits/s and therefore an articulatory-based approach might provide the ultimate in low bit-rate coding of speech, if a technique for extracting the articulatory targets directly from the speech signal could be developed.

One of the most comprehensive articulatory models that has been developed to date is illustrated in figure 5.19. This model was developed by Mermelstein (1973) and represents the vocal-tract outline as a function of ten variables, which specify the position of the jaw, tongue, lips, velum and hyoid. These parameters specify the shape of the vocal-tract outline viewed in the mid-sagittal plane. The position of the jaw and hyoid are expressed directly in fixed co-ordinate systems; the jaw position, J, is specified relative to the fulcrum F through the angle θ_j and the distance S_j and that of the hyoid, H, through the rectangular co-ordinates H_x and H_y. The lip and tongue body positions are specified relative to the moving jaw. The degrees of lip opening and lip protrusion are specified by the parameters L_p and L_h respectively. The tongue body outline is modelled as a circle with a fixed radius, CB, and a moving centre C, specified in relation to the fulcrum and the jaw through the distance S_c and the angle θ_c. The tongue body and tongue blade are considered as separate but inter-dependent articulators with the tongue tip being specified relative to the tongue body through the parameters θ_t and S_t.

The transformation from a vocal-tract outline to a vocal-tract area function involves a two-stage process. Firstly, the mid-sagittal distance is extracted by superimposing a grid over the vocal-tract outline, as shown in figure 5.19(b). The mid-sagittal distance is measured between the intersection of the outlines with the grid-lines. A line is plotted through the centre of these distances and measured to give the vocal-tract length. The mid-sagittal distance function is converted into a cross-sectional area function using transformation equations which take account of the direction of speech propagation, the distance between the centre of the mid-sagittal distances and the three-dimensional shape of the vocal tract.

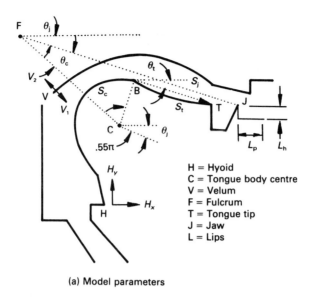

H = Hyoid
C = Tongue body centre
V = Velum
F = Fulcrum
T = Tongue tip
J = Jaw
L = Lips

(a) Model parameters

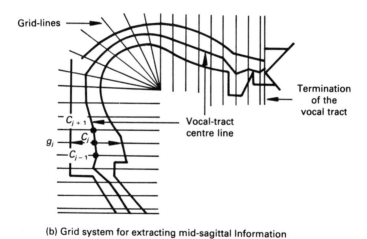

(b) Grid system for extracting mid-sagittal Information

Figure 5.19   Mermelstein's articulatory model, after Mermelstein (1973)

Most acoustic tube models are based on a representation of the vocal
tract as a concatenation of a number (10–40) of uniform, cylindrical tubes,
as shown in figure 5.5. A detailed mathematical analysis of the air-flow and
air-pressure distribution in an acoustic tube, reveals a close analogy to
current and voltage distribution on an electrical transmission line. Thus, it
becomes possible to equate pressure with voltage, flow or volume velocity
(measured in cm³/s), with current, the inertia of the air with inductance,

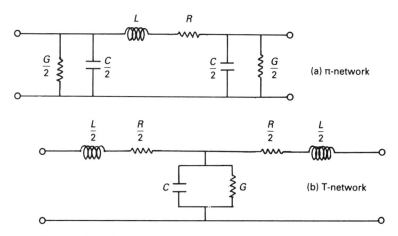

Figure 5.20   Electrical equivalent circuits of vocal-tract section

the air compressibility with capacitance and viscous, and heat-conduction losses with series and shunt resistances. Each tube section can therefore be represented by a lumped electrical transmission line equivalent circuit, as shown in figure 5.20. Either a π- or T-network may be used. The component values depend on such constant quantities as the density of the air and velocity of sound in air, but vary as the cross-sectional area, A, of the tube varies. For example, L is inversely proportional to A, C is directly proportional to A, the viscous loss resistance R is inversely proportional to A^2. The heat-conduction loss G is proportional to the tube circumference. A complicating factor in the case of the viscous and heat-conduction loss components is that strictly they are frequency-dependent; in other words, each frequency component of the air-flow contributes a resistance proportional to the square of its amplitude. Thus, they are not pure components in the electrical sense.

The equivalent circuits in figure 5.20 model a tube with rigid walls. In reality, the vocal-tract walls are constantly vibrating as the pressure inside the tract varies. The energy required to cause this motion is another source of energy loss in the tract. The energy loss due to wall vibration can be modelled in a transmission line model by adding a wall impedance circuit, as shown in figure 5.21. The mass, compliance (stiffness) and damping of the vocal-tract walls are modelled by a series LCR circuit in parallel with the line. The wall loss component, P_w, as communicated to the outside air, is represented as a voltage drop across part of the resistance and inductance.

Another loss mechanism which has to be simulated in an acoustic tube model is that of radiation from the mouth or nostrils. As acoustic energy emanates from the vocal tract, it encounters a radiation impedance, which

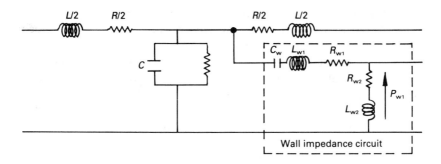

Figure 5.21 Modelling of wall vibration in vocal-tract section

consists of a loss resistance and other inductive and capacitive components. A simple and reasonably accurate model may be obtained if radiation from the mouth is equated to radiation from a vibrating piston in an infinite plane baffle. This can be represented by an equivalent parallel R–L circuit, as shown in figure 5.22.

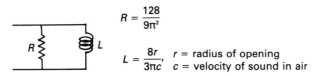

Figure 5.22 Electrical equivalent circuit of radiation from mouth

A complete transmission line model of the vocal tract can therefore be represented by cascading the requisite number of sections of the type shown in figure 5.20 and by terminating them with a radiation model (figure 5.22). The problem then is how to compute the input–output relationship. A variety of solutions have been developed for this problem and they differ mainly in terms of their computational complexity, the detail to which the losses are modelled and whether the input–output relationship is calculated in the time-domain or the frequency-domain. In the latter approach, the overall input–output relationship, including the excitation, is computed in the frequency-domain and the frequency response is then inverse-transformed to obtain the time response. Each section of tract is modelled as a two-port network and its transmission parameters calculated and represented as a (2×2) matrix. The overall frequency of the tract can then be calculated by simply multiplying the chain of matrices together. A so-called hybrid approach has also been adopted. The vocal-tract frequency response has been computed as previously described and then inverse-transformed to obtain the vocal-tract impulse response, which is then convolved with a glottal volume velocity signal to give the output speech signal.

In the time-domain approach, the transfer function of each section is derived and sets of difference equations are used to compute the pressure and flow distribution in every section along the tract. One of the most computationally efficient time-domain models is based on a travelling-wave transmission line. A solution of any transmission line equations clearly shows that there are two propagating waves on the line – a forward-travelling wave and a backward-travelling wave. In the case of the acoustic-tube model represented by sections of line of different characteristic impedances, the section junctions are points of discontinuity and the travelling waves undergo propagation and reflection at these points. The reflection coefficient, r, is given by

$$r = \frac{Z_f - Z_b}{Z_f + Z_b} \tag{5.5}$$

where Z_f is the characteristic impedance forward of the junction and Z_b is the characteristic impedance backward of the junction. At the junction between sections k and $k + 1$, it may be shown that the forward (P^+) and backward (P^-) travelling pressure waves in each section are related by the equations

$$P_{k+1}^+[n] = (1 + r_k)P_k^+[n - 1] - r_k P_{k+1}^-[n] \tag{5.6a}$$

$$P_k^-[n] = r_k P_k^+[n - 1] + (1 - r_k)P_{k+1}^-[n] \tag{5.6b}$$

A complete N-section reflection line model based on the above equations is shown in figure 5.23. For a lossless tube, the values of the reflection coefficients, r_k, are real quantities between ± 1 and thus it is easy to compute samples of the output from samples of the input. Fortunately, it is also possible to model all of the vocal-tract loss mechanisms and still maintain this basic structure. Often the model is represented as internally lossless with lumped terminations, modelling the radiation load, the glottal impedance and losses due to viscous friction and wall-vibration. It is also possible internally to represent viscous loss and wall vibration loss.

Accurate modelling of the excitation sources (voiced and unvoiced) and their interaction with the acoustic-tube model is another important aspect of articulatory speech synthesis. Voiced excitation is caused by the vibrating action of the vocal cords, causing the air-flow from the lungs to be split into pulses which excite the resonances of the vocal tract. Vibration of the vocal cords commences when the sub-glottal pressure is increased beyond a

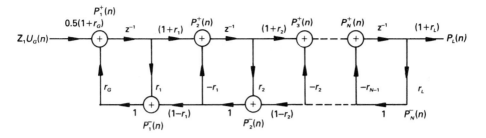

Figure 5.23   Reflection transmission line model of vocal tract

certain value and at the same time the muscular tension on the cords is increased. Assuming the cords are initially together, the pressure increase forces them apart and air flows through the opening. As the air-flow builds up, the local pressure on the cords decreases and the muscular forces cause them to close again. As the cords are drawn together again, the flow diminishes and the local pressure begins to approach the sub-glottal value again. This relaxation cycle repeats itself indefinitely if the sub-glottal pressure and muscular tension are maintained at correct values. The period of oscillation and shape of the glottal waveform is determined by the mass, tension and stiffness of the cords as well as the value of the sub-glottal pressure.

One of the most comprehensive models of vocal cord behaviour is the so-called *two-mass model*, developed by Ishizaka and Flanagan [Flanagan, 1972; Ishizaka and Flanagan, 1972], which models cord vibration and uses the calculated motion to control the characteristics of an electrical equivalent circuit of glottal air-flow. A schematic diagram of this model is shown in figure 5.24. The cords are assumed to be bilaterally symmetrical and therefore the properties of only one cord are shown. The trachea, leading to the lungs, is represented by the pipe to the left. The larynx tube, leading to the vocal tract, is to the right. These two tubes are assumed to be cylindrical in shape and the glottis constitutes a construction between them. The size of the construction is determined by the cord displacement. Each cord is represented by two masses, m_1 and m_2, coupled by a linear spring of stiffness k_c. The function of this coupling spring is to represent an effect of flexural stiffness in the lateral direction of the cords, which results from a human ability to vary the thickness and stiffness of the cords by muscular action. Motion pictures of vocal-cord vibration show that there is a phase difference between the movement of the upper and lower edges of the cords. The use of the two coupled masses for each cord can simulate this effect quite well. The non-linear springs s_1 and s_2 are an equivalent representation of the tension in the vocal cords, which become firmer

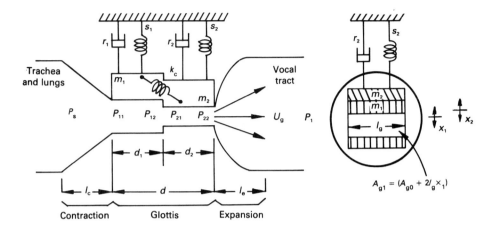

Figure 5.24   Two-mass model of vocal chords, after Ishizaka and Flanagan
(1972)

under muscular contraction. The equations of motion of the two masses
giving them lateral displacements x_1 and x_2 are

$$m_1\ddot{x}_1 + r_1\dot{x}_1 + s_1 + k_c(x_1 - x_2) = f_1 \qquad (5.7a)$$

$$m_2\ddot{x}_2 + r_2\dot{x}_2 + s_2 + k_c(x_2 - x_1) = f_2 \qquad (5.7b)$$

where r_1 and r_2 are the damping resistances, s_1 and s_2 are the non-linear
spring forces and f_1 and f_2 are the forces due to the mean pressure acting on
the masses.

The electrical equivalent circuit of the glottal region is shown in figure
5.25. P_s represents the sub-glottal or lung pressure, which is held essentially constant during speech production by contraction of the lungs. The
time-varying components R_g and L_g represent the equivalent resistance
and inductance of the contraction glottis and expansion (figure 5.24). Both
these components are functions of the glottal opening and hence of the
displacement of the masses m_1 and m_2; R_g is also dependent on the glottal
flow U_g. P_t denotes the pressure at the input to the vocal tract and the
dependence of the airflow U_g on this value models the natural cord/tract
interaction. With reference to the equivalent circuit in figure 5.25, it can be
seen that the glottal volume velocity U_g satisfies the following differential
equation:

$$R_gU_g - L_g\dot{U}_g = P_s - P_t \qquad (5.8)$$

Many of the parameters in the differential equations (5.7) and (5.8) are

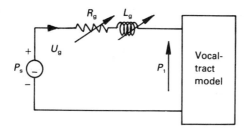

Figure 5.25 Equivalent circuit of glottal region

clearly inter-dependent but, with certain approximations, they can be solved simultaneously to obtain the mass displacements and the glottal volume-velocity U_g. The main parameters, which are used to control the frequency (pitch) of the glottal air-flow, are the lung pressure and the stiffness of the vocal cords.

Accurate modelling of turbulent air-flow for the production of aspiration and frication is probably the most challenging aspect of articulatory speech synthesis. Turbulent air-flow consists of three-dimensional fluctuating eddies of air around a point of constriction in the vocal tract. Because of the additional kinetic energy of the eddies and the additional viscous loss, the energy losses in the tract increase substantially and vary randomly with the flow. The problem is therefore to determine automatically in the model when turbulence occurs, to model the turbulence and the increased energy loss.

Automatic detection of turbulent flow is normally carried by keeping track of the variation of the local *Reynolds' number* for the flow in each element of the acoustic tube. Turbulence occurs in a particular element if the local Reynolds' number rises above a critical value. The squared Reynolds' number, Re^2, is given by

$$Re^2 = \frac{4p^2|U_{dc}|}{\pi\mu^2 A_c} \tag{5.9}$$

where U_{dc} is the d.c. air-flow, A_c is the area of the constriction, and p and μ are the density and viscosity of air respectively. The turbulent flow itself is modelled by the insertion of a random pressure source, P_{ng}, or a random volume-velocity source downstream from the point of constriction. The intensity of the noise source is often made proportional to the difference of the squared local Reynolds' number, Re^2, and the critical Reynolds' value, Re^2_{crit}, that is

$$P_{ng} \text{ or } U_{ng} = K \cdot random \cdot \{Re^2 - Re^2_{crit}\} \tag{5.10}$$

where K is an amplitude control factor and *random* is a random number uniformly distributed between ±0.5. For frication, a volume-velocity source is normally preferred, since it has been found that its location in relation to the constriction is less critical than for a pressure source. This is normally inserted in the first section after the constriction, as shown in figure 5.26. The increased energy loss due to turbulence is represented by the insertion of an additional kinetic resistance in series with the viscous resistance. The value of this resistance depends on the d.c. flow, and the uniformity and cross-sectional area of the constriction is given by the equation

$$R_t = \frac{Cp|U_{dc}|}{2A_c^2} \tag{5.11}$$

where C is a factor determined by the uniformity of the constriction.

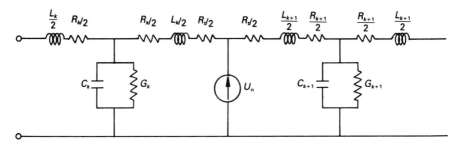

Figure 5.26   Modelling turbulent noise generation in vocal tract

In the case of turbulent flow at the glottis (aspiration), a noise pressure source is added to the pressure difference across the glottis, that is in series opposition to the pressure source P_s in figure 5.25, and the kinetic resistance R_t is inserted in series with R_g.

A number of articulatory synthesisers, based on the above principles, have been developed, and although most are computationally very intensive and are not yet able to emulate the speech quality of conventional synthesisers, it has been demonstrated that they do have the potential for producing very natural-sounding speech. The basic problem currently is the severe lack of data about the relative timings of articulatory movements and about articulatory dynamics. Much work remains to be done.

Problems

5.1. Show that applying the impulse invariant method of digital filter design to the analogue bandpass resonator transfer function in equation (5.1) yields the digital resonator transfer function in equation (5.2).

5.2. Design a digital formant resonator with a centre frequency of 500 Hz and a bandwidth of 120 Hz.

6 Speech Coding

In chapter 2, a number of techniques for efficiently coding the speech signal at bit-rates down to about 16 kbits/s were described. These included log-PCM, adaptive PCM (APCM), differential PCM (ADPCM), delta modulation (DM), adaptive delta modulation (ADM) and continuously variable slope delta modulation (CVSD). All of these techniques operate directly on the time-domain signal and achieve reduced bit-rates by exploiting the sample-to-sample correlation or redundancy in the speech signal.

In this chapter, a number of additional techniques for efficiently coding the speech signal at bit-rates in the range 16 kbits/s down to less than 1 kbit/s are described. In all of these techniques, a modified or transformed version of the speech signal is coded rather than the time-domain signal itself.

A number of frequency-domain coding techniques are also discussed, in which the speech signal is transformed into the frequency-domain, encoded and transmitted. An inverse process in the receiver converts the frequency-domain encoded signal back into the time-domain. These frequency-domain coders can be classified as either parametric or non-parametric. Parametric coders are often referred to as Vocoders (from *voice coders*) or analysis/synthesis coders and incorporate an analysis stage for extracting a set of parameters which represent separately the vocal-tract excitation signal and the vocal-tract spectral envelope. These parameters are encoded and transmitted to the receiver where they are used to control a synthesis stage which reconstructs the original speech signal. In non-parametric coders no attempt is made to separate out the excitation and vocal-tract information.

Parametric coders can give good speech quality at bit-rates down to 2.4 kbits/s. The performance of non-parametric coders deteriorates substantially at bit-rates below about 9.6 kbits/s. However, the performance of parametric coders does not increase indefinitely with bit-rate; above about 9.6 kbits/s no perceptual improvement in speech quality can be obtained.

A very important class of speech coders, called linear predictive coders (LPC) is also described. An LPC coder is a time-domain parametric coder in which a time-varying parametric representation of the speech signal is derived by computing a set of linear predictor coefficients, or related coefficients (section 4.2), and a set of excitation parameters, at discrete instants in time. These parameters are encoded according to perceptual criteria, transmitted and decoded at the receiver in order to recover the original signal. LPC coders can operate with reasonable quality down to bit-rates of the order of 2.4 kbits/s.

6.1 Sub-band coding

In the various time-domain coding techniques described in chapter 2 (log-PCM, ADPCM etc.) the input signal is the full-bandwidth signal. In sub-band coding, the input signal is first split into a number of frequency bands by bandpass filtering and then the output signal from each filter is coded using one or a combination of the techniques described in chapter 2. The filter outputs are largely uncorrelated and the redundancy in the input speech signal is removed. The bit allocation in the encoding of the various sub-bands is based on perceptual criteria; for example, it is beneficial to encode the low-frequency end of the spectrum more accurately than the high-frequency end. An added advantage is that the quantisation noise in each band is fixed with no noise interference between bands.

The block diagram of a general sub-band coder is given in figure 6.1. The digitised input signal is filtered by a set of N bandpass filters which cover the frequency range of interest, for example, 300–3400 Hz for telephone speech. Typically 2–5 bands are used. The output of each bandpass filter is heterodyned to base-band (low-pass translated) by multiplying it with a sinusoid whose frequency is equal to the amount of shift (translation) required. This process is equivalent to single-sideband amplitude modulation and effectively converts the signal from a bandpass signal to a low-pass signal with the same bandwidth. Since each low-pass signal has a much smaller bandwidth than that of the original signal, its sample rate can be considerably reduced. This is achieved through a decimation process $(D_n:1)$, which simply involves retaining every D_nth sample of the filter output and discarding D_n-1 samples. The decimation factor D_n is determined by the bandwidth of the filter and the sample rate of the original speech signal. Bearing in mind Nyquist's sampling theorem, and using ideal bandpass filters, it is easy to show that

$$D_n = f_s/2b_n \tag{6.1}$$

where f_s is the input signal sample rate and b_n is the bandwidth of the nth bandpass filter.

Each sub-band is quantised and encoded using one of the many techniques outlined in chapter 2. Typically, adaptive PCM (APCM) is used for this but sometimes ADPCM and ADM are employed. The coded sub-bands are then multiplexed and transmitted along the communications

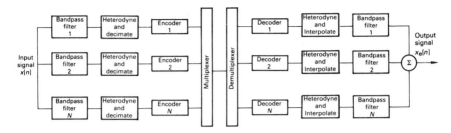

Figure 6.1   Sub-band coder

channel or are stored for later retrieval in the case of speech storage systems. At the receiver, an inverse sequence of events takes place. The sub-bands are demultiplexed and decoded and then each sub-band signal is interpolated by inserting zeros to replace the samples discarded during decimation at the receiver. Each signal is heterodyned back to its original band and is then bandpass-filtered using an identical response to the corresponding filter in the transmitter. All bandpass filter outputs are summed together to reproduce the original signal.

Table 6.1 gives a typical sub-band partitioning for a family of sub-band coders operating at 16, 24 and 32 kbits/s. The input sampling rate is 8 kHz and 5 sub-bands are used to cover the frequency band of interest, which is 0–4 kHz in this case. As shown in the table, the 0–1000 Hz region of the spectrum is split into two sub-bands using bandpass filters, each with a bandwidth of 500 Hz and a corresponding decimation factor and sampling rate of 8 and 1000 Hz respectively. The 1–4 kHz region is split into a further three sub-bands, using 3 bandpass filters, each with a bandwidth of

Table 6.1   Typical sub-band coder characteristics (sampling rate – 8 kHz; speech frequency band, 0–4 kHz)

Band	Filter band edges	Decimation factor	Sub-band sample rate (Hz)	Sub-band bit allocation (bits/s amp) at bit-rate (kbits/s) of		
				16	24	32
1	0–500	8	1000	4	5	5
2	500–1000	8	1000	4	5	5
3	1000–2000	4	2000	2	4	4
4	2000–3000	4	2000	2	3	4
5	3000–4000	4	2000	0	0	3

2 kHz and a corresponding decimation factor and sampling rate of 4 and 2000 Hz respectively. The bit assignment for the output of each sub-band, corresponding to bit-rates of 16, 24 and 32 kbits/s, is shown in the three rightmost columns. Note that the total bit-rate in each case is obtained by summing the product of sampling rate and bit assignment for each sub-band.

Sub-band coding can be used for coding speech at bit-rates in the range 9.6–32 kbits/s. In this range, speech quality is roughly equivalent to that of ADPCM at an equivalent bit-rate. In addition, its complexity and relative speech quality at low bit-rates makes it particularly advantageous for coding below about 16 kbits/s. However, the increased complexity of sub-band coding compared with other techniques probably does not warrant its use at bit-rates in excess of about 20 kbits/s.

6.2 Transform coding

Transform coding is a frequency-domain coding technique, in which a short-time transformation of the signal is efficiently coded by assigning more bits to more important transform coefficients than to less important coefficients. At the receiver, an inverse transformation is used to reconstruct the speech signal. In order to reflect the non-stationarity of the speech signal, the transform coefficients are updated at regular time-intervals, for example 10–20 ms.

A number of different methods can be used to obtain the spectral transformation, including the discrete Fourier transform described in section 3.3. However, a related transform, called the discrete-cosine transform (DCT) is more efficient and more appropriate in transform coding. The DCT is defined by the following relations:

$$X(k) = \alpha(k) \sum_{n=0}^{N-1} x[n] \cos\{(2n+1)k\pi/N\}, \quad k = 0, 1, \ldots, N-1 \quad (6.2a)$$

$$x[n] = \frac{1}{N}\alpha(k) \sum_{n=0}^{N-1} X(k) \cos\{(2n+1)k\pi/N\}, \quad n = 0, 1, \ldots, N-1 \quad (6.2b)$$

where $\alpha(k) = 1, \quad k = 0,$
$\qquad\qquad = 2^{1/2}, \, k = 1, 2, \ldots, N-1,$
$x[n]$ denotes a windowed speech segment of length N samples and $X(k)$ denotes the transform coefficients.

Typical segment lengths are 128–256 samples. Equation (6.2a) can be written in matrix form as

Signal Processing of Speech

$$X(k) = A(k, n) \cdot x(n), \quad A(k, n) = \alpha(k) \cos\{(2n+1)k\pi/N\} \qquad (6.3)$$

where $X(k)$ and $x(n)$ are column matrices of dimension N, representing the transform coefficients and the windowed input signal respectively, and $A(k, n)$ is a square $(N \times N)$ transformation matrix. At the receiver, the original signal is recovered by multiplying the transform coefficient vector by the inverse of this transformation matrix. In the case of the DCT the transformation matrix is unitary, which means it has the special property that its inverse is equal to its transpose. This means that the inverse is simply obtained by interchanging the rows and columns. In practice, the matrix multiplication can be speeded up by computing the DCT via the DFT, using an FFT algorithm. This involves extending the length of the original N-point sequence to $2N$, by folding it so that it possesses even symmetry, taking a $2N$-point FFT and retaining the first N terms of it. This approach is valid because the DFT of a real symmetric sequence produces a sequence which contains only real coefficients, corresponding to the cosine terms of the series.

Most practical transform coding systems for speech are adaptive in the sense that although the total number of bits available to quantise the transform coefficients remains constant, the bit allocation to each coefficient changes from frame to frame. This dynamic bit allocation is controlled by the time-varying statistics of the speech, which have to be transmitted as side information. Figure 6.2 [after Zelinski and Noll, 1977] is a block diagram of a complete adaptive transform coder (ATC). The frame of N samples to be transformed or inverse-transformed is accumulated in the buffer in the transmitter and the receiver respectively. The side information is also used to determine the step-sizes of the various coefficient quantisers. In a practical system, the side information transmitted is a coarse representation of the log-energy spectrum. This typically consists of L frequency points, where L is in the range 15–20, which are computed by averaging sets of N/L adjacent squared values of the transform coefficients $X(k)$. At the receiver, an N-point spectrum is reconstructed from the L-point spectrum by geometric interpolation, which is equivalent to linear interpolation in the log-domain. The number of bits assigned to each transform coefficient is proportional to its corresponding spectral energy value. The encoding of the side information requires of the order of 2 kbits/s.

Adaptive transform coding (ATC) can be used to encode speech successfully at bit-rates in the range 9.6 kbits/s to 20 kbits/s. Its complexity is somewhat higher than that of sub-band coding.

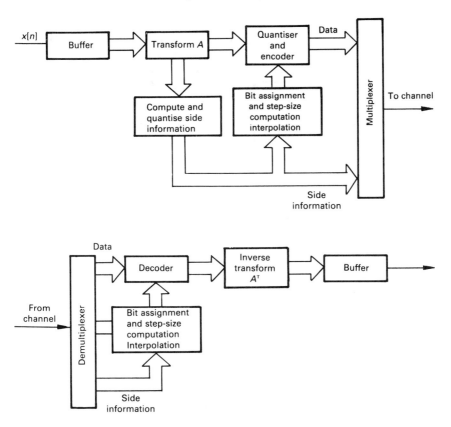

Figure 6.2   Adaptive transform coder, after Zelinski and Noll

6.3 Channel Vocoder

The basic principle of the Channel Vocoder has already been described in the brief outline of the history of speech synthesis in section 5.1. The Channel Vocoder is a parametric frequency-domain coder and consists of both an analyser and a synthesiser, as shown in figure 6.3. The analyser consists of a number of bandpass filters (typically 16–19), covering the speech frequency band of interest (0–4 kHz say), whose outputs are rectified and smoothed (low-pass filtered). The specification (centre frequencies and bandwidths) of a 19-channel Vocoder analyser was given in table 3.1 (section 3.2). The filter outputs are synchronously sampled every 10–30 ms, thereby deriving the short-time amplitude spectrum of the speech signal, which is multiplexed with a voiced/unvoiced decision and the pitch frequency for voiced speech and transmitted to the receiver. Pitch

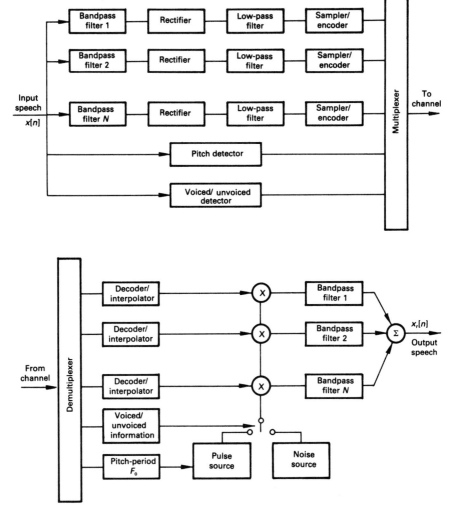

Figure 6.3   The Channel Vocoder

extraction and the voiced/unvoiced decision would typically be extracted using one of the algorithms described in chapter 4.

At the receiver, the excitation and vocal-tract information is demultiplexed. The excitation information is used to switch in a random noise or a pulse source and to set the frequency of the pulse source. The received signal in each channel is used to modulate the amplitude of the excitation signal which excites the corresponding bandpass filter. The bandpass filter outputs are summed to produce the synthesised signal. The centre fre-

Table 6.2　Details of Marconi Channel Vocoder

Number of channels	19
Audio frequency range	240–3600 Hz
Sampling rate	10 kHz
Pitch extraction	Gold–Rabiner
Frame period	20 ms (50 frames/s)
Bit allocation	
pitch	6 bits
V/UV	1 bit
Channel 1	3 bits (6 dB step-size)
Channels 2–9	2 bits/channel DPCM (± 3, ± 9 dB)
Channels 10–19	1 bit/channel, DPCM (± 6 dB)
Error protection	12 bits (optional)
Total bits	48

quencies of the filters used in the synthesiser are identical to those in the analyser, though the bandwidths are substantially less.

A practical Channel Vocoder might have a number of enhancements to the basic structure given in figure 6.3. For example in the Marconi Channel Vocoder, the logarithm of the filter outputs are taken and encoded using a delta PCM (DPCM) technique. Automatic gain control (AGC) is used to maximise the efficiency in the encoding of the first channels and all other channels are encoded relative to this one by transmitting the difference between the present channel and the last channel coded. Some of the details of the Marconi Channel Vocoder [Kingsbury and Amos, 1980] are given in table 6.2. The number of bits allocated to the excitation and vocal-tract parameters is 36 bits/frame or 1800 bits/s. An additional 12 bits/frame (600 bits/s) are allocated for error protection, which greatly improves performance when the Vocoder is operating over a noisy communications channel.

6.4 Formant vocoder

In the discussion of formant synthesisers in the previous chapter (section 5.2), it was indicated that a formant synthesiser, either serial or parallel, is capable of producing very high-quality speech when driven by an appropriate set of parameters (typically 10–20), that is the time-varying frequencies, amplitudes and bandwidths of the vocal-tract resonances and pitch and voicing information. Formant parameters are small in number, vary relatively slowly with time and have a relatively small dynamic range. They can be efficiently and accurately coded at bit-rates down to around 1 kbit/s.

A formant vocoder therefore consists of an analyser, which extracts the time-varying formant and excitation parameters automatically from the speech signal. These are then encoded and passed to the synthesiser, where they are decoded and used to control a formant synthesiser, which reconstructs the original signal. From the description of formant tracking algorithms in section 4.5, it is clear that automatic extraction of the formant frequency values is fraught with problems. Although a number of formant vocoders have been built, they have not been entirely successful because of the formant-tracking problem. However, the technique still holds a lot of promise for the future. In fact, the performance of formant vocoders has been substantially improved through the use of neural networks (section 7.5.3), to smooth the formant tracks.

6.5 Cepstral vocoder

The principles of cepstral analysis were discussed in section 3.5. This speech processing technique involves separating the excitation and vocal-tract spectrum by inverse Fourier-transforming the log-magnitude spectrum to produce the cepstrum of the signal. The low-frequency coefficients in the cepstrum correspond to the vocal-tract spectral envelope with the high-frequency excitation coefficients forming a periodic pulse train at multiples of the sampling period. The vocal-tract cepstral coefficients are separated from the excitation coefficients by a linear filtering operation, which involves multiplying the cepstral coefficients by an appropriate window function. This retains only the low-frequency excitation coefficients (figure 3.18). The time-position of the first pulse in the cepstrum gives the pitch-period of the excitation signal and the presence or absence of a strong pulse indicates whether the speech is voiced or unvoiced. The block diagram of a cepstral vocoder is given in figure 6.4. In the analyser, the cepstral coefficients are derived as described above and these, together with the pitch and voicing parameters, are encoded and transmitted to the synthesiser. In the receiver (synthesiser) the vocal-tract cepstral coefficients are Fourier-transformed, exponentiated and inverse Fourier-transformed to produce the vocal-tract impulse response. By convolving this impulse response with a synthetic excitation signal (random noise or a periodic pulse train), the original speech is re-constructed.

6.6 Linear predictive vocoders

The basic technique of linear predictive analysis (LPA) and linear predictive synthesis was discussed at some length in sections 3.7 and 5.3, respectively. The basic idea of linear prediction is that any speech sample $x[n]$ can

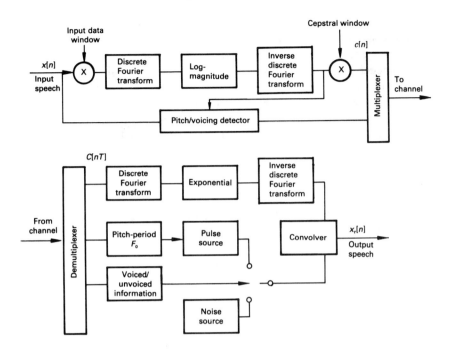

Figure 6.4   Cepstral vocoder

be approximated as a linear combination of the previous p samples, where p is typically in the range 10–15. The predicted sample $\tilde{x}[n]$ is given by

$$\tilde{x}[n] = \sum_{k=1}^{p} a_k x[n-k] \tag{6.4}$$

where the predictor coefficients a_k are chosen to minimise the mean-squared error $\overline{e^2[n]}$ between the actual signal and the predicted signal. Calculation of a set of predictor is normally carried out every 10–30 ms by solving a set of linear equations, using either the autocorrelation or the covariance algorithms.

The original speech signal can be re-constructed exactly from the predictor coefficients if the error signal is known, that is

$$x[n] = e[n] + \tilde{x}[n]$$

$$= e[n] + \sum_{k=1}^{p} a_k x[n-k] \tag{6.5}$$

This equation leads to an LPC speech synthesiser, depicted in figure 5.14, in which the vocal tract is modelled by the all-pole linear predictor and the excitation signal $e[n]$ is modelled by a 'stylised' error signal, $G \cdot u[n]$, where G is a gain parameter and $u(n)$ is a unit sample generator in the case of voiced speech and a random number generator $(-1 \leqslant u[n] \leqslant +1)$ in the case of unvoiced speech.

In linear predictive synthesis, quantisation of the prediction coefficients can lead to instability of the synthesis filter and for this reason, it is preferable to use a lattice synthesis filter (figure 5.15). The so-called reflection coefficients of the lattice filter are bounded in the range ± 1 and have much superior quantisation and stability properties. However, it has been observed that the LPC frequency spectrum is very sensitive to quantisation errors in reflection coefficients close to $+1$ or -1. In order to alleviate this problem, a non-linear transformation of the reflection coefficients has been proposed which gives a new set of coefficients, called the log-area ratios (LARs), for which the spectral sensitivity is small and constant. The log-area ratios are defined by

$$\text{LAR}_i = \log \frac{1 + r_i}{1 - r_i}, \, i = 1, 2, \ldots, p \tag{6.6}$$

and are so called because the ratio $(1+r_i)/(1-r_i)$ gives the ratio of the cross-sectional areas of adjacent sections in an equivalent acoustic-tube model of the vocal tract consisting of a number of discrete cylindrical tubes [Markel and Gray, 1976]. The reflection coefficients can be obtained from the log-area-ratios by simply inverting equation (6.6), that is

$$r_i = \frac{e^{\text{LAR}i} - 1}{e^{\text{LAR}i} + 1} \tag{6.7}$$

In speech coding applications involving quantisation and encoding of predictor parameters, the log-area-ratios are the optimum parameters to use.

6.6.1 The LPC-10 algorithm

The LPC-10 algorithm is a US standard for linear predictive coding of speech at 2400 bits/s. The synthesis model is a 10th-order lattice filter, controlled by a set of 10 reflection coefficients which are updated pitch-synchronously every 22.5 ms. There are 54 bits assigned to encode the parameters in each 22.5 ms frame and this gives rise to the bit-rate of 2400 bits/s. The sampling rate is 8 kHz and the covariance algorithm is used for the linear predictive analysis. Semi-pitch-synchronous analysis is employed in that not all of the samples in each frame are used in the analysis. A fixed duration analysis interval of approximately 16 ms is used and the beginning of the implied rectangular window is placed at the maximum point of

Table 6.3   Main features of LPC-10 speech coding Algorithm

Bit-rate – 2400 bits/s
Sampling rate – 8 kHz
Frame length – 22.5 ms
LPC Analysis – Semi-pitch-synchronous covariance algorithm
Model order – 10 (voiced speech); 4 (unvoiced speech)
Coding parameters – reflection coefficients:
                     log-area-ratios (r_1 and r_2);
                     linear (r_3–r_{10})
Gain G – r.m.s. signal value
Pitch extraction – AMDF algorithm

Bit allocation	Voiced	Unvoiced	
Pitch	7	7	(pitch – 6 bits; V/UV – 1 bit)
Gain, G	5	5	
r_1	5	5	
r_2	5	5	
r_3	5	5	
r_4	5	5	
r_5	4	–	
r_6	4	–	
r_7	4	–	
r_8	4	–	
r_9	3	–	
r_{10}	2	–	
Synchronisation	1	1	
Error protection	–	21	
Total (bits/frame)	54	54	

excitation within each frame. The main parameters and features of the LPC-10 algorithm are summarised in table 6.3. Some additional points are worth noting. For voiced speech a stylised glottal pulse is stored in the synthesiser and replicated at intervals of the pitch-period. This gives an improvement in speech quality over the standard periodic unit-sample generator. In the case of unvoiced speech, a 4th-order model is used rather than a 10th-order one, since the spectrum of unvoiced sounds can be adequately represented by the lower-order model. The spare bits in unvoiced frames are used for error protection. The gain parameter G is given by the r.m.s. value of the signal in the analysis frame. Log-area-ratios are used for the coding of the first two reflection coefficients and standard linear coding for the remainder.

The speech produced by the LPC-10 coding algorithm (2400 bits/s) is of good, though less than telephone, quality. The main defect is its perceived robotic quality, which can often disguise the identity of the speaker. This is generally accepted as being due to the simplistic modelling of the excitation. A number of schemes for improving the model of excitation will be discussed in the following sub-sections.

6.6.2 Multi-pulse and RELP vocoders

Since the linear prediction error or residual signal $e[n]$ can be obtained by inverse-filtering and used to re-construct the original signal exactly, it follows that if this signal could be encoded accurately and efficiently, a good-quality Vocoder system should result. This is the principle used in two types of vocoder, known as the multi-pulse vocoder and the residual excited linear predictive (RELP) vocoder. Such systems have an additional advantage, in that they do not require a pitch estimator or a voiced/ unvoiced detector.

The residual signal has a smaller dynamic range than the speech signal itself and thus, fewer bits are required to encode it. However, direct encoding only gives a slight reduction in the bit rate, because on occasions, the dynamic range of the error signal can approach that of the speech signal itself. A more efficient scheme for encoding the residual signal is therefore required.

In multi-pulse LPC, each frame of the residual signal is represented by a skeleton residual signal, which consists of typically 8–10 non-zero samples (pulses), whose amplitudes and positions within a frame are chosen in such a way as to keep the perceptually-weighted error between the synthesised speech and the original speech as small as possible. Perceptual weighting is applied to de-emphasise the spectrum of the error signal in the formant frequency ranges; errors in the formant ranges are masked by the high concentration of energy around formant frequencies and are perceptually less important than in-between formant errors.

The position and amplitude of the pulses can be obtained using an analysis by synthesis procedure, as depicted in figure 6.5. For a given frame of speech, the procedure begins with zero excitation and a signal is produced because of the energy stored in the LPC synthesis filter from previous frames. This signal is then subtracted from the original speech signal to produce an error signal which is then filtered using the perceptual weighting filter. The position and amplitude of a single pulse are then determined so as to minimise the mean-squared weighted error. A new error signal is then computed using the new estimate of the excitation and the process is repeated until the positions and amplitudes of all the pulses have been determined. Multi-pulse LPC can almost produce 8-bit log-PCM quality speech at around 9.6 kbits/s, though 6-bit log-PCM quality systems operating at 4.8 kbits/s have been successfully implemented.

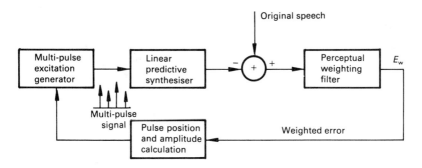

Figure 6.5   Block diagram of multi-pulse LPC coding system

The LPC residual has a spectrum which is relatively broad and flat and the base-band component below about 1 kHz contains most of the significant information. In the residual-excited linear predictive (RELP) approach to speech coding, only the base-band component of the residual signal is encoded and transmitted. At the receiver, the full-bandwidth residual signal is re-generated and used as the excitation signal for the LPC synthesiser. A significant saving in bit-rate can be achieved, since fewer bits are required to model the base-band signal compared with the full-bandwidth signal. Like multi-pulse LPC, pitch and voicing estimators are not required.

The base-band signal may be either time-domain or frequency-domain encoded. In the time-domain approach, the residual is low-pass filtered using a filter with a cut-off frequency in the range 800–1000 Hz and then decimated, typically by a factor of 4:1 or 5:1. The filtered signal is then waveform-coded using, for instance, adaptive PCM (APCM) or adaptive delta modulation (ADM) and transmitted, along with the linear predictive coefficients, to the synthesiser. At the receiver, the residual base-band signal is first interpolated back to its original sample-rate and then an attempt is made to regenerate as accurately as possible, the full-bandwidth signal. This can be achieved reasonably successfully by a non-linear operation, such as full-wave rectification of the base-band signal, followed by a double-differencing of the signal, to obtain a flat spectrum.

Alternatively, the residual signal may be encoded in the frequency-domain. This involves computing the spectrum of the residual signal, using the FFT for example, and then transmitting the low-frequency end (below about 1 kHz). At the receiver, the spectrum of the full-bandwidth spectrum is obtained by repeatedly copying the base-band component the requisite number of times. An inverse-transformation is then carried out, in order to recover the complete time-domain residual signal. The success of this approach depends on the accuracy of the copy-up procedure in preserving the original harmonic structure of the residual. One problem is that, in general, the harmonics of the residual signal will not be properly spaced at the 'joints' between adjacent copies of the base-band spectrum, that is at 1 kHz, 2 kHz, 3 kHz etc. for a 1 kHz base-band component. This leads to the presence of additional tones in the output speech, which cause minor distortion. The effect can be reduced by allowing the base-band cut-off frequency to vary, so that the last harmonic of pitch occurs exactly at the edge of the band. This, however, necessitates the calculation and transmission of pitch, so that the spectrum can be folded about the appropriate point in the receiver and also increases the data-rate.

RELP coding is typically used at bit-rates around 9.6 kbits/s, though successful systems operating down to 4.8 kbits/s have been implemented.

6.7 Vector quantiser coders

An important class of speech coders for reasonable coding of speech at low bit-rates (less than 1 kbits/s) are those based on vector quantisation. The idea of vector quantisation which was discussed in section 4.4 is that, instead of quantising the speech analysis parameters (linear prediction coefficients, spectral coefficients, filter-bank energies etc.) individually, a codebook is set up, consisting of a finite set of M vectors, covering the anticipated range of the parameter values. In each analysis interval, the codebook is searched and the entry which gives the best match to the speech input frame is selected.

In speech coding systems employing vector quantisation, identical codebooks of the appropriate vectors are stored in both the transmitter and the receiver. Thus, there is only a requirement to transmit the address of the codebook entry, rather than the vector itself. This requires substantially fewer bits. For example, a large codebook with 1024 vectors only requires 10 bits/frame ($2^{10} = 1024$). Vector-quantiser-based coding systems operating only at a few hundred bits per second are capable of producing reasonably good-quality speech.

One of the greatest difficulties with this type of coding is in setting up a good-quality codebook; significant amounts of training are involved. In addition, there is a need for very efficient algorithms to search the codebook, as this can take a significant amount of processing time at the encoding stage. However, many efficient algorithms for searching codebooks have been developed.

In the case of linear predictive systems, vector quantisation can also be applied to the LPC residual as well as to the LPC coefficients themselves. This leads to another class of LPC coders, known as code-excited linear predictive coders. In CELP coding, the residual signal is coded, using a codebook containing typically 2^{10} (1024) short segments of residual waveform. Although CELP systems can produce telephone-quality speech at

4.8 kbits/s, their complexity makes them less attractive than multi-pulse coders.

A suitable text for further reading on the topic of Speech Coding is the book by Papamichalis [1987].

7 Automatic Speech Recognition

For many years, speech recognition by machine existed only in the minds of science-fiction writers. However, in recent years, the real problem of automatic speech recognition (ASR) has been addressed in many research laboratories throughout the world. The ultimate goal of this research is to produce a machine which will recognise accurately normal human speech from any speaker. Such a machine could be used in a wide variety of applications including speech input to computers, office automation, factory automation, security systems, aids for the handicapped, consumer products and almost any job involving hands-busy/eyes-busy activities. In an ever-expanding information technology and advanced telecommunications age, speech recognition and synthesis devices would permit remote access to a wide variety of information services over the telephone.

Unfortunately, the problem of automatic speech recognition is proving much more difficult than perhaps was first appreciated, with the result that it is still far from being completely solved, despite much research effort. Nevertheless, this research has resulted in the development of a number of limited speech recognition systems which perform reasonably well in some applications.

The aim of this chapter is to outline some of the difficulties encountered in ASR and to describe the main techniques that are currently being used in speech recognition systems.

7.1 Problems in ASR

In chapter 1 it was indicated that simplistically speech may be considered as a sequence of sounds, taken from a set of fifty or so basic sounds called phonemes. Different sounds are produced by varying the shape of the vocal tract through muscular control of the speech articulators (lips, tongue, jaw etc.). However, very wide acoustic variations occur when the same phoneme is spoken by different people, because of differences in the vocal apparatus. For example, differences in vocal-tract length and musculature account for the deeper-sounding male voice and the higher-pitched female one. Moreover, the same individual may produce acoustically different versions of the same sound from one rendition to the next. In fast speech, individual speech sounds can become very short in duration or perhaps even be left out entirely. Also, we normally anticipate what we are about to say. Hence, when articulating one phoneme, the vocal apparatus prepares for the next one. These anticipatory movements alter the acoustics of the phoneme being spoken. This is referred to as co-articulation which is one of the greatest obstacles in automatic speech recognition.

Another significant problem is the fact that there are no identifiable boundaries between sounds or even words. Even the relatively simple task of determining where an utterance begins and ends (endpoint detection) presents problems and is error-prone, particularly in noisy operating conditions.

Another problem is variability due to differences in dialect which often includes leaving out certain sounds (phone deletion) or replacing one sound with another (phone substitution). Prosodic features such as intonation, rhythm and stress also cause variability in the speech signal. In addition the speech signal may contain speech-related noises such as lip smacks, tongue clicks, and breathing noises, ambient noise from the speaker's surroundings and perhaps telephone-like noise if the speech recognition system is being used over the telephone.

The speech signal itself cannot always convey all of the acoustic–phonetic information required to decode it. Speech utterances are subject to syntactic and semantic constraints and a human uses these sources of knowledge to help anticipate words. High-performance speech recognition systems will probably only be developed when these high-level processes are fully understood and incorporated.

In order to currently realise practical automatic speech recognition systems, the number of variations with which they have to contend is minimised by allowing only a limited vocabulary of words, by restricting the sequence of words using an artificial language, by reducing the number of speakers and by requiring the user to speak each word from the vocabulary as an isolated entity. Depending on the extent of this minimisation, the recognition system may be classified as speaker-dependent or speaker-independent and isolated-word or connected-word. A speaker-dependent system is trained to a single speaker's voice by obtaining and storing patterns for each vocabulary word uttered by that speaker. In a speaker-independent system an 'average' pattern for each vocabulary word is stored so that any speaker can use the system without the need for training. In an isolated-word system each vocabulary word must be spoken in isolation with distinct pauses between words whereas in connected-word systems no pauses are necessary. Continuous speech recognition systems also do not require pauses between words but have at least medium-sized vocabularies (> 1000 words) and permit the input of complete sentences.

7.2 Dynamic time-warping (DTW)

In this section a class of speech recognition systems based on acoustic pattern matching is discussed. The success of these recognisers depends largely on the power of a technique called dynamic time-warping (DTW) which takes some account of the time-scale variation referred to in the previous section.

7.2.1 Isolated word recognition

In isolated word recognition systems the acoustic pattern or template of each word in the vocabulary is stored as a time sequence of features (frames), derived using one of the speech analysis techniques described in chapters 3 and 4. Recognition is performed by comparing the acoustic pattern of the word to be recognised with the stored patterns and choosing the word which it matches best as the recognised word. A block diagram of a basic isolated word recognition system is illustrated in figure 7.1. In order to obtain reasonably acceptable performance and to keep the amount of processing within reasonable limits, the number of words to be matched must be quite small (< 100). In a speaker-dependent system the stored patterns are acquired during a training session when a potential user is required to utter each word in the vocabulary. The system is then really only suited to that user's voice. In a speaker-independent system, an 'average' set of patterns is previously stored in the system and, in general, no training is required. Some systems are speaker-adaptive in that they continuously adapt the stored templates to a given user as he or she successfully uses the system. This can substantially increase the recognition performance.

7.2.2 Pattern matching

The function of the pattern matching block of the isolated-word speech recognition system in figure 7.1 is to determine the similarity between the input word pattern and the stored word patterns. This involves not only distance computation but also time-alignment of the input and reference patterns because a word spoken on different occasions, even by the same speaker, will exhibit both local and global variation in its time-scale. The simplest method of time-aligning two patterns of unequal length is to map the time-axis of one onto the time-axis of the other in a linear fashion as shown in figure 7.2(a). It is clear that this method is not entirely satisfactory since it does not guarantee that the internal parts of the patterns will be properly aligned although it does give proper alignment of the beginning and end of the patterns. What is really required is an alignment function which properly matches the internal features of the pattern as

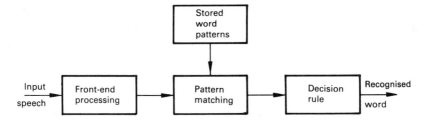

Figure 7.1   Basic isolated-word recognition system

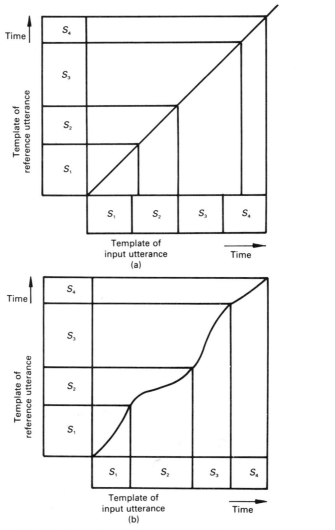

Figure 7.2   (a) Illustration of linear time alignment of utterances;
(b) illustration of non-linear time alignment (dynamic time-warping)

shown in figure 7.2(b). Much of the computational effort in speech pattern matching is in deriving a near optimal alignment function. This can be achieved by a technique called dynamic time-warping (DTW) which will now be discussed.

Let $P_1(n)$, $n = 1, 2, \ldots, N$, and $P_2(m)$, $m = 1, 2, \ldots, M$, denote the two patterns to be matched. P_1 and P_2 consist of N and M frames respectively of a multi-dimensional feature vector. The time-alignment of these two patterns is illustrated in figure 7.3 where, for simplicity, the two patterns are shown as one-dimensional functions. It is assumed that both the beginning and end points of the two patterns have been accurately determined. The goal is to find an alignment curve which maps $P_1(n)$ onto corresponding parts of $P_2(m)$. In other words, an alignment function of the form $m = \omega(n)$ is required, which relates the n time-axis of P_1 to the m time-axis of P_2. The constrained beginning and end points in figure 7.3 can formally be expressed as constraints on $\omega(n)$, that is $\omega(1) = 1$ and $\omega(N) = M$. For any two patterns, $\omega(n)$ is that function or path which minimises the distance between them. In mathematical terms, $\omega(n)$ can be determined by solving the optimisation problem expressed as

$$D^* = \text{Min} \left\{ \sum_{n=1}^{N} d[P_1(n), P_2(\omega(n))] \right\} \qquad (7.1)$$

where $d[P_1(n), P_2(\omega(n))]$, is the distance between frame n of P_1 and frame $\omega(n)$ of P_2, and D^* is the accumulated distance between P_1 and P_2 over the optimal path $\omega(n)$. The solution to this problem may be found by a technique called dynamic programming which was first applied in the design of optimal control systems.

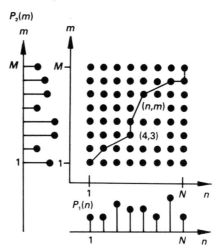

Figure 7.3   Time-alignment of two one-dimensional patterns

Dynamic programming is a technique used in multi-stage decision processes where decisions are made at discrete time-intervals during the course of some transaction in which the outcome of the transaction is a function of all the decisions. The set of rules for making decisions throughout a particular process is called a policy; and a policy which results in an optimal process is called an optimal policy. Fundamental to the method of dynamic programming is the 'principle of optimality' which states – 'An optimal policy has the property that, whatever the initial state and initial decision may be, the remaining decisions must constitute an optimal policy with respect to the state resulting from the first decision'. In other words the last part of an optimal process is itself an optimal process. The principle of optimality applied to the pattern-matching framework of figure 7.3 may be stated as follows – 'If the best path from the grid-point (1, 1) to the general grid-point (n, m) goes through the grid-point (4, 3), for example, then the best path from (1, 1) to (4, 3) is part of the best path from (1, 1) to (n, m)'. In other words, the optimum global path can be obtained by always locally choosing the path which minimises the distance between the two patterns.

In addition to the endpoint constraints mentioned above, a number of other restrictions are placed on the time-alignment path. For example, it would generally be unrealistic to permit a path which resulted in excessive compression or expansion of the time-scale. Another obvious restriction is that the slope of the path can never be negative, that is time-order must be preserved by making $\omega(n)$ increase monotonically. These local constraints are incorporated by specifying the full path in terms of simple local paths which may be pieced together to form larger paths. Figure 7.4 gives two typical examples of local paths. In figure 7.4(a) the path to the grid-point (n, m) can only come from one of three points, that is $(n, m-1)$, $(n-1, m-1)$ or $(n-1, m)$. The local path illustrated in figure 7.4(b) differs from that in figure 7.4(a) in that one of the valid paths is different. It also has a non-linear constraint which dictates that the path to the point (n, m) from $(n-1, m)$ is valid only if the previous path to $(n-1, m)$ did not come from $(n-2, m)$. In other words the optimal path cannot be flat for two consecutive frames.

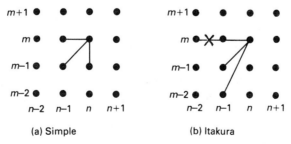

(a) Simple   (b) Itakura

Figure 7.4   Typical local path constraints

If $D_A(n, m)$ denotes the minimum accumulated distance along any path from the grid-point $(1, 1)$ to the grid-point (n, m), then, using the local path constraint in figure 7.4(a), $D_A(n, m)$ can be computed recursively using dynamic programming, that is

$$D_A(n, m) = d[P_1(n), P_2(m)] \tag{7.2}$$
$$+ \text{Min } \{D_A(n, m-1), D_A(n-1, m-1), D_A(n-1, m)\}$$

The above equation indicates that the minimum accumulated distance from the grid-point $(1, 1)$ to the grid-point (n, m) consists of the local distance between frame n of pattern P_1 and frame m of pattern P_2 plus the minimum of the accumulated distances to the grid-points $(n, m-1)$, $(n-1, m-1)$ and $(n-1, m)$. Equation (7.2) forms the basis of a dynamic time-warping algorithm for pattern matching in speech recognition. Initially $D_A(1, 1)$ is set equal to $d[P_1(1), P_2(1)]$, that is the local distance between the first frames of the two patterns. Then $D_A(n, m)$ is computed sequentially for all values of n and m in the range $n = 1$ to N and $m = 1$ to M. Finally, the accumulated distance D^* over the optimal path is given by $D_A(N, M)$. The optimum time-alignment path $\omega(n)$ can be determined by backtracking from the end of the path, although for most speech recognition applications only the optimal accumulated distance is required and computation of the actual warping path is of no benefit.

Figure 7.5 illustrates the use of the above dynamic time-warping algorithm to compute the distance between two one-dimensional patterns $P_1 = \{1, 6, 9, 6, 5\}$ and $P_2 = \{2, 6, 8, 9, 8, 3\}$ using the so-called 'city-block' distance measure:

$$D(P_1, P_2) = \sum_i |P_1(i) - P_2(i)| \tag{7.3}$$

Firstly, a local distance matrix is drawn up as shown in figure 7.5(a) by taking the magnitude of the difference between each frame in P_1 and every frame in P_2. For example, the entry in column 2, row 3 of the matrix, that is 2, gives the local distance between frame 2 of P_1 and frame 3 of P_2, that is $|8 - 6| = 2$. The accumulated distance matrix in figure 7.5(b) is computed by applying equation (7.2). For example, the entry in column 3, row 3 is the accumulated distance to the grid-point $(3, 3)$ which is equal to the local distance between frame 3 of P_1 and frame 3 of P_2 plus the minimum of the accumulated distances to the points $(3, 2)$, $(2, 2)$ and $(2, 3)$, that is $1 + \text{Min} \{4, 1, 3\} = 2$. The total distance between the two patterns over the optimal path is the distance in the top right-hand corner of the accumulated-distance matrix, that is 6. The time-alignment path may be obtained by backtracking from the top right-hand corner of the accumulated-distance matrix as shown in figure 7.5(b). During backtracking the next point on the

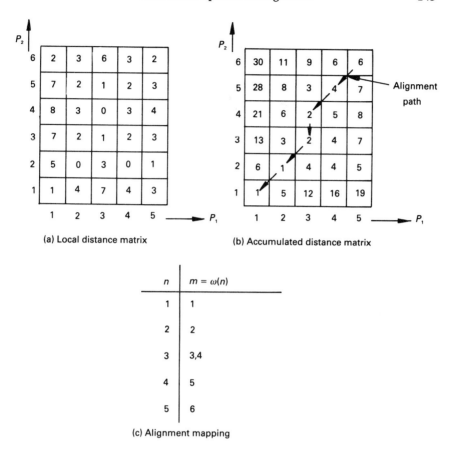

(a) Local distance matrix

(b) Accumulated distance matrix

n	$m = \omega(n)$
1	1
2	2
3	3,4
4	5
5	6

(c) Alignment mapping

Figure 7.5 Illustration of dynamic time warping

path is given by that point at which the accumulated distance to the three possible surrounding points is a minimum. The complete time-alignment function $\omega(n)$ is given in figure 7.5(c). Note that frame 3 of pattern P_1 is mapped onto both frame 3 and frame 4 of pattern P_2

It is possible to specify many different forms of local path constraint other than that shown in figure 7.4(a). The so-called Itakura constraint illustrated in figure 7.4(b) produces a DP algorithm which performs very well and is used in many speech recognition systems. An interesting property of this algorithm is that it gives rise to a well-defined region in which all possible alignment paths may lie. This region which is a parallelogram bounded by sides of slope 2 and slope $\frac{1}{2}$ as illustrated in figure 7.6. The slope constraint of $\frac{1}{2}$ is determined by the condition that the optimal path cannot be flat for two consecutive frames and the slope constraint of 2 is

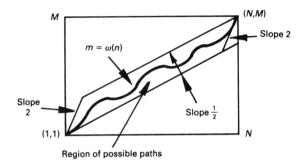

Figure 7.6   Path region for Itakura local path constraint

determined by the condition that no path to the grid-point (n, m) can come from any point lower than $(n-1, m-2)$. This knowledge can be used to increase the efficiency of the algorithm since there is no point in computing accumulated distances at points outside the parallelogram and the storage requirements are also reduced. Both of these are very important since dynamic time-warping algorithms are computationally expensive to implement and the storage requirements, especially for large vocabularies, can be substantial. In fact, most speech recognition systems based on dynamic time-warping use some form of adjustment window to restrict the region in which the alignment path may lie. There are a number of different methods for computing the width of the adjustment window but it is generally made inversely proportional to the difference in duration of the words being matched.

7.2.3 Speaker-independent recognition

In a speaker-independent speech recognition system there is no training and so the stored word patterns must be representative of speakers who will use the system. The word templates are normally derived by first obtaining a large number of sample patterns from a cross-section of talkers of different sex, age-group and dialect, and then clustering these to form a representative pattern for each word. A representative pattern can be created by averaging all the patterns in a word cluster. A dynamic time-warping algorithm would normally be employed to compute a time-alignment function which takes some account of the different time-scales. A much simpler approach is to select a representative pattern from the middle of each cluster. However, because of the great variability in speech, it is generally impossible to represent each word cluster with a single pattern and so each cluster is normally broken up into sub-clusters and a number of tokens for each vocabulary word is stored in the system. This may be as many as ten or twelve, though obviously the greater the number then the greater the computation involved at the recognition stage since all tokens of each word will have to be matched against the input word.

7.2.4 Pattern classification (decision rule)

The last stage in the speech recognition system in figure 7.1 is a pattern classification stage which is basically a rule for deciding which stored pattern most closely matches the input pattern. Although a variety of rules may be used, the most widely used one is known as the nearest-neighbour (NN) rule. Suppose there are N stored patterns in the system, R_i, $i = 1, 2, \ldots , N$, and the distance D_i between the input pattern and each stored pattern is computed, then the best match R_i^* according to the nearest-neighbour rule may be computed from

$$i^* = \operatorname*{argmin}_{i} [D_i] \qquad (7.4)$$

That is, choose the pattern R_i^* with the smallest average distance as the recognised word. In speaker-independent systems with multiple tokens for each word, a modified rule known as the K-nearest-neighbour rule is often used. With this rule, the vocabulary word whose average distance of the K nearest neighbours to the input word is minimum is chosen as the recognised word.

7.2.5 Connected-word recognition

Since it is highly unnatural to have always to speak with distinct pauses between the words, a number of DTW-based algorithms have been developed which can cope with strings of words which are spoken in connected groups. One example is the speaking of connected digits such as telephone numbers, bank-account numbers etc. The most obvious approach would be to try to segment the connected word string into distinct words and then recognise these as before, but segmentation cannot be done reliably because of co-articulation effects between words. At first sight, an alternative approach might be to concatenate isolated word patterns to form all possible combinations of connected word patterns and then apply a dynamic time-warping algorithm to find the sequence of word patterns which best matches the connected input pattern. However, even for moderately sized vocabularies and for small connected strings, this approach is impractical because of the amount of computation involved. For example, a system, with a vocabulary consisting of the ten digits 0 to 9 and capable of recognising up to a maximum of four-digit numbers spoken in a connected fashion, would have to match a total of 10^4 four-digit patterns plus 10^3 three-digit patterns plus 10^2 two-digit patterns plus 10 one-digit patterns! Some algorithms which reduce the amount of computa-

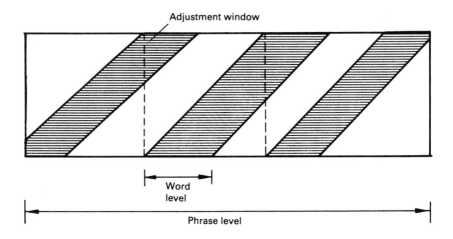

Figure 7.7   Two-Level DTW connected-word algorithm

tion to reasonably manageable proportions will now be described.

One of the first algorithms for connected-word recognition was a two-level dynamic programming algorithm consisting of a word-level matching stage followed by a phrase-level matching stage [Sakoe, 1979]. In the word-level stage, each stored word pattern is matched against all possible regions in the connected-word input pattern as shown in figure 7.7. An adjustment window is used to define a region in which each word in the connected-word pattern may start and end. This gives rise to a matrix of partial distances. In the phrase-level stage, dynamic programming is performed on the partial distances to obtain the sequence of words which gives rise to the minimum total distance.

A more efficient algorithm is the so-called *level-building algorithm* [Myers and Rabiner, 1981]. In this algorithm, dynamic time-warping is applied at a number of stages or levels up to the maximum number of anticipated words in the connected-word string. The process is illustrated in figure 7.8 for the simple case of a four-word vocabulary (W, X, Y and Z) and an input string of known length 4. The use of the Itakura local path constraint gives rise to the parallelogram window which indicates the region in which the warping path lies. In level 1, each stored word pattern is matched against the beginning of the input string using dynamic time-warping which proceeds in the normal way for each value of n sequentially in the valid range, that is $N_1 \leq n \leq N_2$. Then the distance scores to the top row of grid-points for each word pattern is examined and, for each valid ending frame in level 1, the best scoring pattern is noted as shown together with the accumulated distance for that pattern. These form the initial

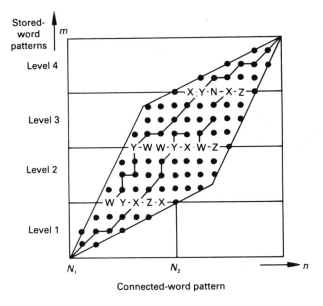

Figure 7.8   Illustration of level building algorithm

accumulated distances for the next level. For each best-scoring pattern, a record is also kept of a backtracking pointer which points to the starting position (value of n) of the path to each cell at the end of the current level. For level 1, it is clear that $n = 1$ since, in level 1, all paths must originate at the grid-point (1, 1). At this point, the best estimate of the first spoken word in the string and its ending position within the utterance may be obtained by finding the position n of the best of the lowest scoring patterns. This may or may not be eventually chosen as the first word in the spoken string.

In subsequent levels, dynamic time-warping proceeds in a similar way with the best scoring accumulated distances to the grid-points at the end of the preceding level forming the initial conditions. In order to determine the backtracking pointers for the best-scoring patterns at all possible ending points, it is necessary to backtrack. This determines the starting positions at the previous level of the sub-path to each grid-point at the end of the current level. When the anticipated number of levels have been added (built), the sequence of words in the string is determined by backtracking from the top right-hand grid-point using the backtracking pointers. If the number of words in the input string is not known, the distances to the top right-hand grid-points in each level can be compared to find the best estimate of the number of words in the string. If the lowest of these distances is at level L, then it may be estimated that there are L words in the string.

From the qualitative description of the level building algorithm given above, it is clear that three basic quantities must be computed. These are: (i) the best minimum accumulated distance

$$D_L^*(n) = \underset{1 \leqslant V \leqslant N}{\text{Min}} \{D_L^V(n)\} \tag{7.5}$$

where $D_L^V(n)$ is the accumulated distance for the Vth word pattern at level L, ending at frame n of the input pattern, and N is the number of vocabulary words to be matched at level L; (ii) the best word pattern

$$W_L(n) = \underset{1 \leqslant V \leqslant N}{\text{Argmin}} \{D_L^V(n)\} \tag{7.6}$$

where Argmin denotes the value of the index which minimises the expression, that is the word pattern leading to the minimum accumulated distance; (iii) a backtracking pointer, $P_L(n)$, which contains the frame number of the input pattern at level $L-1$ from which the sub-path for the best scoring reference at that point originated.

Another algorithm for connected-word recognition is the *one-stage* or *Bridle* algorithm [Bridle *et al.*, 1983]. Each word pattern is matched against a first portion of the input pattern using a dynamic time-warping algorithm and a few of the best scoring patterns together with their corresponding ending positions in the input pattern are recorded. Then each word pattern is matched against the second portion of the input pattern starting at the points where the last word matches ended. This process is repeated until the end of the input pattern is reached and generates what is called a word-decision tree as shown in figure 7.9 which 'grows' as the input is processed. After the first match vocabulary words W_4, W_6 and W_3, ending at frames 10, 32, and 22 respectively, are selected as possible ways of explaining the first part of the unknown input pattern. Some paths are eventually ended as better-scoring paths are found. When all of the input pattern has been processed the unknown word sequence is obtained by tracing back through the tree. Unlikely paths are eliminated when their accumulated distances are more than some specified amount greater than the best-scoring path and a number of likely paths are carried along in parallel. This type of approach is often referred to as a *beam search*. It avoids considering unlikely interpretations of the input pattern but keeps the options open if there is some ambiguity. It also leads to a considerable reduction in computation.

The recognition performance for the two-level algorithm, the level-building algorithm and the one-stage algorithm is more or less the same for the same task. However, it has been shown that the computation and storage requirements of each are substantially different. The one-stage algorithm requires only about 25 per cent of the computation required by the level-building algorithm and only about 4 per cent of that of the two-level algorithm. The one-stage algorithm requires only about 10 per

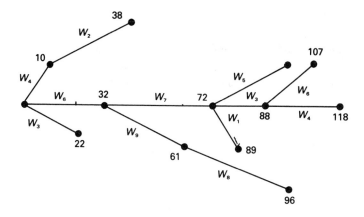

Figure 7.9 Illustration of one-stage algorithm

cent of the storage requirements of the other two algorithms. All of the algorithms have been been implemented in real-time in a number of speech recognition systems.

So far in our study of connected-word recognition algorithms, the assumption is that any of the vocabulary words can follow any other. Sometimes in speech recognition applications there is some knowledge of the order in which the vocabulary words will be spoken. In this sort of situation, it is possible to represent allowable strings of words using a directed graph or syntax tree structure as shown in figure 7.10 for an airline booking system. Junctions between words are called 'nodes'. Such a struc-

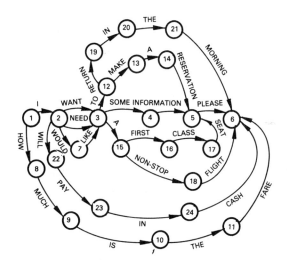

Figure 7.10 Example of a state diagram representation of a regular language

ture can be used to reduce significantly the number of word patterns that need to be matched at any given point in the input pattern. This greatly reduces the amount of computation and also enhances the recognition performance of the system. Finite-state syntaxes are, however, limited; they do not have the richness of structure of the natural language that we use conversationally.

7.3 Hidden Markov models

A powerful technique for modelling the temporal structure and variability in speech is one called *hidden Markov modelling*. This is a probabilistic pattern-matching approach which models a time-sequence of speech patterns as the output of a stochastic or random process. The hidden Markov model (HMM) consists of an underlying Markov chain as illustrated in figure 7.11. Each of the six circles represents a state of the model and at a discrete instant in time t, corresponding to the frame time, the model is in one of these states and outputs a certain speech pattern or *observation*. At time instant $t + 1$, the model moves to a new state, or stays in the same state, and emits another pattern. This process is repeated until the complete sequence of patterns has been produced. Whether it stays in the same state or moves to another state is determined by probabilities, $\{a_{ij}\}$, associated with each transition, where $\{a_{ij}\}$, denotes the probability of moving from state i at time t to state j at time $t + 1$. Note that in any state the sum of the probabilities of staying in that state or moving to another state is 1.0. In any state, the production by the model of a speech pattern, drawn from a finite set of M patterns using the technique of vector quantisation (section 4.4), is also governed by a set of probabilities, $\{b_{jk}\}$, as illustrated in figure 7.11, where $\{b_{jk}\}$ denotes the probability of producing pattern k when the model is in state j. The starting state of each model is also uncertain and this is represented by a probability $\{\pi_j\}$ which denotes the probability of the model being in state j at time $t = 0$. Obviously, the sum of the π probabilities across all the states should equal 1. For the model in figure 7.11, the starting state is either the first or the second with an equal probability of each.

The model is said to be 'hidden' in that the state sequence that produced a given sequence of patterns cannot be determined. Also, in a general HMM, a transition from a state to any other state is possible, but the model in figure 7.11 is 'left-to-right' in that no backwards transitions are allowed. This is necessary in order to model the temporal structure of speech effectively. Other left-to-right models, with different numbers of states and different topologies, are also appropriate for modelling speech patterns though they are not significantly better or worse than that shown in figure 7.11.

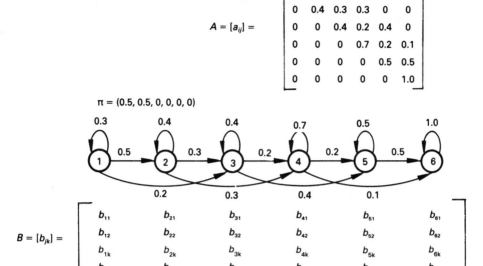

$$A = [a_{ij}] = \begin{bmatrix} 0.3 & 0.5 & 0.2 & 0 & 0 & 0 \\ 0 & 0.4 & 0.3 & 0.3 & 0 & 0 \\ 0 & 0 & 0.4 & 0.2 & 0.4 & 0 \\ 0 & 0 & 0 & 0.7 & 0.2 & 0.1 \\ 0 & 0 & 0 & 0 & 0.5 & 0.5 \\ 0 & 0 & 0 & 0 & 0 & 1.0 \end{bmatrix}$$

$\pi = (0.5, 0.5, 0, 0, 0, 0)$

$$B = [b_{jk}] = \begin{bmatrix} b_{11} & b_{21} & b_{31} & b_{41} & b_{51} & b_{61} \\ b_{12} & b_{22} & b_{32} & b_{42} & b_{52} & b_{62} \\ b_{1k} & b_{2k} & b_{3k} & b_{4k} & b_{5k} & b_{6k} \\ b_{1M} & b_{2M} & b_{3M} & b_{4M} & b_{5M} & b_{6M} \end{bmatrix}$$

Figure 7.11   Example of a hidden Markov model (HMM)

A better understanding of the operation of a Markov model in producing a sequence of speech patterns may be obtained by considering a simple analogy. Six containers numbered 1 to 6 contain counters of various colours. There are ten different colours and each container contains unequal numbers of each colour. A coin is initially tossed to determined which container to start with ('heads' = container 1, 'tails' = container 2) and a counter is drawn at random from the selected container. Its colour is noted and it is then replaced. A dice is thrown to determine which box to select next and a counter is again drawn at random, its colour noted and it is again replaced. The dice is repeatedly thrown until say fifty colours have been noted.

In this simple analogy, the containers correspond to states and the sequence of states is determined by the throwing of the dice. The tossing of the coin gives an equal probability of either container 1 or container 2 being initially selected, that is $\{\pi_j\} = \{0.5, 0.5, 0, 0, 0, 0\}$. In selecting the next container at any stage in the process, there is an equal probability of 1/6 that either the present container will be selected again or one of the five other containers will be selected. The 6×6 matrix $\{a_{ij}\}$ in this case will have all its elements equal to 1/6. The probability $\{b_{jk}\}$ of a particular colour of counter, k, being drawn from a particular container, j, depends on the relative number of each colour in that container which varies from container to container. Therefore in this particular case, the state-pattern –

probability – matrix $\{b_{jk}\}$ will have a dimension of (6×10), since there are 6 states (containers) and 10 patterns (colours). The sequence of colours of the drawn counters corresponds to the frame sequence of speech patterns or *observation sequence*. In the case of the simple coloured counters analogy, the process could be described as 'hidden', if an observer of the event was not made aware of the identity (number) of each container.

It is perhaps not immediately obvious how a hidden Markov model can be related to the process of speech production. Simplistically, speech is a sequence of different sounds, produced by the speech articulators taking up a sequence of different positions. If we regard the articulatory positions corresponding to static sounds as states, then speech can be viewed as the result of a sequence of articulatory states of different and varying duration. Hence the transitions between states can be represented by probabilities, $\{a_{ij}\}$, and the overall Markov chain represents the temporal structure of the word. The acoustic patterns or observations produced in each state correspond to the sound being articulated at that time. Because of variations in the shape of the vocal apparatus, pronunciation etc., the production of these patterns may also be represented by probabilistic functions $\{b_{jk}\}$.

Obtaining a model for each vocabulary word involves iteratively adjusting the two probability functions so as to maximise the likelihood that the training sequence of patterns could be produced by that model. Large amounts of training data are required in order to produce good word models. For speaker-dependent systems this would involve several repetitions of each word and for speaker-independent systems several repetitions of each word by several speakers. The speech recognition phase involves computing the likelihood of generating the unknown input pattern with each word model and selecting the word model that gives the greatest likelihood as the recognised word. This is known as *maximum likelihood classification*. The amount of computation involved in recognition is substantially less than that in training. The recognition and training problems will be considered in more detail shortly.

The recognition accuracy of a speech recognition system based on hidden Markov modelling is slightly better than that of an equivalent system based on dynamic time-warping though its storage and computation requirements would be roughly an order of magnitude less. In a HMM system it is much easier to capture and model speaker variability although, as has already been pointed out, this involves substantial training computation. In addition, the technique of hidden Markov modelling can be applied to sub-word units, such as syllables, demi-syllables, phones, diphones and phonemes, and thus seems to have the potential for implementing large-vocabulary, speaker-independent systems.

7.3.1 Word recognition using HMMs

A block diagram of a complete isolated-word recognition system based on hidden Markov modelling is shown in figure 7.12. The word to be recognised is suitably endpointed, split into a time sequence of T frames and analysed using some speech analysis procedure, such as filter bank, fast Fourier transform (FFT), linear predictive analysis (LPA) etc. This produces a sequence of observations O_t, $t = 1, 2, \ldots, T$, which are vector-quantised using a codebook containing a representative set of M speech patterns P_k, $k = 1, 2, \ldots, M$. Then the likelihood of producing the unknown input word pattern with each of the W word models is computed. The input word is recognised as that model which produces the greatest likelihood.

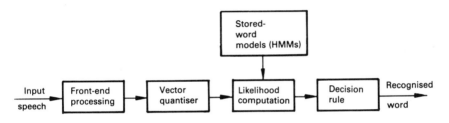

Figure 7.12   HMM-based isolated word recognition system

Mathematically speaking, each word model M_i, $i = 1, 2, \ldots, W$, is defined by the parameter set $[\pi, A, B]$ where $\pi = \{\pi_i\}$ is a column matrix denoting the probability of the model starting in state i, $A = \{a_{ij}\}$ is a square matrix denoting the probability of the model transferring from state i at time t to state j at time $t + 1$ and $B = \{b_{jk}\}$ is a column matrix denoting the probability of the model producing pattern P_k in state j. The likelihood of each model M_i having produced the observation sequence O_t is obtained by computing $Pr_i\{O_t|M_i\}$, that is the probability of the observation sequence O_t given model M_i. The recognised word RW is then given by

$$RW = \operatorname*{Argmax}_{i = 1, 2, \ldots, W} [Pr_i\{O_t|M_i\}] \tag{7.7}$$

where Argmax denotes the value of the argument which maximises the expression.

The problem of computing $Pr\{O|M\}$ will now be considered. The most obvious way of doing this is to consider all possible state sequences that could have produced the observation sequence and then determine that sequence which gives the highest probability. However, this approach is totally unrealistic because of the very large number of sequences involved. In general, there will be N^T sequences, where N is the number of states in the model and T is the number of frames in the observation sequence. Fortunately, $Pr\{O|M\}$ can be calculated using a recursive procedure which reduces the amount of computation to manageable proportions. Two recursive algorithms have been developed: one is called the Baum–Welch algorithm and the other is called the Viterbi algorithm. Both of these will now be discussed.

The *Baum–Welch algorithm* is based upon calculating a set of so-called *forward probabilities*, $\alpha_t(j)$, which are the joint probabilities of emitting the partial observation sequence $O_1, O_2, \ldots, O_t$ and being in state j at time t, that is

$$\alpha_t(j) = Pr\{O_1, O_2, \ldots, O_t, \text{state } j \text{ at time } t|M\}, j = 1, 2, \ldots, N \quad (7.8)$$

The probability of emitting the entire observation sequence of length T and being in state j is $\alpha_T(j)$. Therefore the total probability of emitting the observation sequence, $Pr\{O|M\}$, may be obtained by summing $\alpha_T(j)$ across all N states. When $Pr\{O|M\}$ is computed in this way it is referred to as the *Baum–Welch probability* P^{BW} and is given by

$$P^{\text{BW}} = \sum_{j=1}^{N} \alpha_T(j) \quad (7.9)$$

Suppose $\alpha_T(i)$, $i = 1, 2, \ldots, N$ has been computed at some instant in time t, then the probability of having emitted the partial observation sequence $O_1, O_2, \ldots, O_t$, occupying state i and transferring to state j at time $t + 1$ is $\alpha_t(i) \cdot a_{ij}$. Hence the probability of having emitted the partial observation sequence $O_1, O_2, \ldots, O_t$ and occupying state j at time $t + 1$ may be obtained by summing $\alpha_t(i) \cdot a_{ij}$ across all states, that is

$$Pr\{O_1, O_2, \ldots, O_t, \text{state } j \text{ at } t + 1|M\} = \sum_{i=1}^{N} \alpha_t(i)a_{ij} \quad (7.10)$$

Taking into account the observation O_{t+1} produced by state j at time $t + 1$, then the recursive equation for the forward probability $\alpha_{t+1}(j)$ is given by

$$\alpha_{t+1}(j) = \left\{ \sum_{i=1}^{N} \alpha_t(i)a_{ij} \right\} \cdot b_j(O_{t+1}), \, t = 1, 2, \ldots, T-1 \quad (7.11)$$

where $b_j(O_{t+1})$ is the probability of producing observation O_{t+1} from state j and is obtained from pattern probabilities $\{b_{jk}\}$, that is $b_j(O_{t+1}) = b_{jk}$ when O_{t+1} is vector-quantised to pattern P_k.

The recursion in equation (7.11) is initialised by computing $\alpha_1(j)$ which is the probability of producing the first observation and being in state j at time $t = 1$, that is

$$\alpha_1(j) = \pi\{j\}b_j(O_1) \tag{7.12}$$

In computing the Baum–Welch probability, P^{BW}, using the recursion in equation (7.11), calculation of the forward probability at time $t + 1$ for each state ($\alpha_{t+1}(j)$) involves summing the forward probabilities for all states at time t, and hence P^{BW} is the likelihood of emitting the observation O, summed over all possible state sequences. An alternative algorithm is the Viterbi algorithm which computes the likelihood P^V of the most likely state sequence emitting the observation. P^V can be computed using a dynamic programming algorithm and, if required, the most likely state sequence can be obtained by backtracking.

The likelihood P^V can be obtained by computing $\phi_t(j)$ where

$$\phi_{t+1}(j) = \underset{i = 1, 2, \ldots, N}{\text{Max}} \{\phi_t(i)a_{ij}\}\cdot b_j(O_{t+1}), \ t = 1, 2, \ldots, T-1 \tag{7.13}$$

Equation (7.13) is identical to equation (7.11), except that the summation has been replaced by the Max operator and the algorithm is initialised using equation (7.12) with α replaced by ϕ. The probability of producing the observation sequence O is then given by

$$P^V = \underset{j = 1, 2, \ldots, N}{\text{Max}} \{\phi_T(j)\} \tag{7.14}$$

In general, the Viterbi probability P^V is less than or equal to the Baum–Welch probability P^{BW}. P^V will equal P^{BW} only if the observations can be produced by a unique state sequence. It is also possible to recover the most likely state sequence. This requires recording of the parameter $\mu_t(j)$ which denotes the most likely state of time $t-1$ given state s_j at time t. Hence $\mu_t(j)$ is equal to the right-hand side of equation (7.13) with the Max operator replaced by Argmax, that is $\mu_t(j)$ is the value of i which maximises the equation. Note that the values of $\mu_1(j)$ are not required in the computation since they refer to a time before the start of the observation sequence.

When ϕ and μ have been calculated for all $j = 1, 2, \ldots, N$ and $t = 1, 2, \ldots, T$, the most likely state sequence is obtained by backtracking through the data. The most likely state at time T is state s_k where k is equal to that value of j which maximises equation (7.14). Therefore the most likely state at time $T-1$ is $\mu_T(k)$. The value of $\mu_{T-1}(k)$ gives the most likely state at time $T-2$ and so on until the most likely state at time $t = 1$ is recovered. The basic principles of both the Baum–Welch and Viterbi algorithms are illustrated by the following simple example.

Three urns (1, 2, 3) contain three different colours of counter {red (R), green (G), blue (B)} and a sequence of counters is drawn at random from the urns, the colour of each is noted, and the counter is then replaced. Assume that this process is represented by a hidden Markov model as illustrated in figure 7.13. The problem is to determine the probability of generating the colour sequence red, green, green, blue, red, blue using (i) the Baum–Welch algorithm and (ii) the Viterbi algorithm.

Computation of the solution to the problem is initialised by computing the forward probabilities $\alpha_1(j)$ which is the joint probability of obtaining the first colour and being in state j at time $t = 1$. These are obtained from the initial state probabilities $\pi(j)$ and the probabilities of obtaining the first red (R) counter from each of the three urns, that is

$$\alpha_1(j) = \pi(j) \cdot b_j(O_1)$$

and so

$$\alpha_1(1) = \pi(1) \cdot b_1(R) = 0.8 \times 0.3 = 0.24$$
$$\alpha_1(2) = \pi(2) \cdot b_2(R) = 0.2 \times 0.1 = 0.02$$
$$\alpha_1(3) = \pi(3) \cdot b_3(R) = 0.0 \times 0.4 = 0.0$$

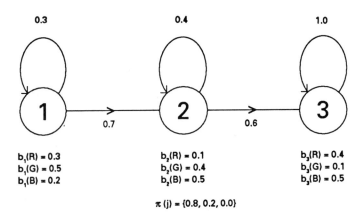

$$\pi(j) = \{0.8, 0.2, 0.0\}$$

Figure 7.13   HMM for coloured counters example

The forward probabilities at successive time instants can now be computed iteratively using equation (7.11):

$$\alpha_2(1) = \{\alpha_1(1) \cdot a_{11} + \alpha_1(2) \cdot a_{21} + \alpha_1(3) \cdot a_{31}\} \cdot b_1(G)$$
$$= \{(0.24 \times 0.3) + (0.02 \times 0.0) + (0.0 \times 0.0)\}0.5$$

$$= \{0.036 + 0.0 + 0.0\}$$
$$= 0.036$$

$$\alpha_2(2) = \{\alpha_1(1) \cdot a_{12} + \alpha_1(2) \cdot a_{22} + \alpha_1(3) \cdot a_{32}\} \cdot b_2(G)$$
$$= \{(0.24 \times 0.7) + (0.02 \times 0.4) + (0.0 \times 0.0)\}0.4$$
$$= \{0.0672 + 0.0032 + 0.0\}$$
$$= 0.0704$$

$$\alpha_2(3) = \{\alpha_1(1) \cdot a_{13} + \alpha_1(2) \cdot a_{23} + \alpha_1(3) \cdot a_{33}\} \cdot b_3(G)$$
$$= \{(0.24 \times 0.0) + (0.02 \times 0.6) + (0.0 \times 1.0)\}0.1$$
$$= \{0.0 + 0.0012 + 0.0\}$$
$$= 0.0012$$

$$\alpha_3(1) = \{\alpha_2(1) \cdot a_{11} + \alpha_2(2) \cdot a_{21} + \alpha_2(3) \cdot a_{31}\} \cdot b_1(G)$$
$$= \{(0.036 \times 0.3) + (0.0704 \times 0.0) + (0.0012 \times 0.0)\}0.5$$
$$= \{0.0054 + 0.0 + 0.0\}$$
$$= 0.0054$$

$$\alpha_3(2) = \{\alpha_2(1) \cdot a_{12} + \alpha_2(2) \cdot a_{22} + \alpha_2(3) \cdot a_{32}\} \cdot b_2(G)$$
$$= \{(0.036 \times 0.7) + (0.0704 \times 0.4) + (0.0012 \times 0.0)\}0.4$$
$$= \{0.01008 + 0.011264 + 0.0\}$$
$$= 0.021344$$

$$\alpha_3(3) = \{\alpha_2(1) \cdot a_{13} + \alpha_2(2) \cdot a_{23} + \alpha_2(3) \cdot a_{33}\} \cdot b_3(G)$$
$$= \{(0.036 \times 0.0) + (0.0704 \times 0.6) + (0.0012 \times 1.0)\}0.1$$
$$= \{0.0 + 0.004224 + 0.00012\}$$
$$= 0.004344$$

$$\alpha_4(1) = \{\alpha_3(1) \cdot a_{11} + \alpha_3(2) \cdot a_{21} + \alpha_3(3) \cdot a_{31}\} \cdot b_1(B)$$
$$= \{(0.0054 \times 0.3) + (0.021344 \times 0.0) + (0.004344 \times 0.0)\}0.2$$
$$= \{0.000324 + 0.0 + 0.0\}$$
$$= 0.00324$$

$$\alpha_4(2) = \{\alpha_3(1) \cdot a_{12} + \alpha_3(2) \cdot a_{22} + \alpha_3(3) \cdot a_{32}\} \cdot b_2(G)$$
$$= \{(0.0054 \times 0.7) + (0.021344 \times 0.4) + (0.004344 \times 0.0)\}0.5$$

$= \{0.00189 + 0.0042688 + 0.0\}$

$= 0.0061588$

$\alpha_4(3) = \{\alpha_3(1){\cdot}a_{13} + \alpha_3(2){\cdot}a_{23} + \alpha_3(3){\cdot}a_{33}\}{\cdot}b_3(\text{G})$

$= \{(0.0054 \times 0.0) + (0.021344 \times 0.6) + (0.004344 \times 1.0)\}0.5$

$= \{0.0 + 0.0064032 + 0.002172\}$

$= 0.0085752$

$\alpha_5(1) = \{\alpha_4(1){\cdot}a_{11} + \alpha_4(2){\cdot}a_{21} + \alpha_4(3){\cdot}a_{31}\}{\cdot}b_1(\text{R})$

$= \{(0.000324 \times 0.3) + (0.0061588 \times 0.0)$

$+ (0.0085752 \times 0.0)\}0.3$

$= \{0.00002916 + 0.0 + 0.0\}$

$= 0.00002916$

$\alpha_5(2) = \{\alpha_4(1){\cdot}a_{12} + \alpha_4(2){\cdot}a_{22} + \alpha_4(3){\cdot}a_{32}\}{\cdot}b_2(\text{R})$

$= \{(0.000324 \times 0.7) + (0.0061588 \times 0.4)$

$+ (0.0085752 \times 0.0)\}0.1$

$= \{0.00002268 + 0.000246352 + 0.0\}$

$= 0.000269032$

$\alpha_5(3) = \{\alpha_4(1){\cdot}a_{13} + \alpha_4(2){\cdot}a_{23} + \alpha_4(3){\cdot}a_{33}\}{\cdot}b_3(\text{R})$

$= \{(0.000324 \times 0.0) + (0.0061588 \times 0.6)$

$+ (0.0085752 \times 1.0)\}0.4$

$= \{0.0 + 0.001478112 + 0.000343008\}$

$= 0.00182112$

$\alpha_6(1) = \{\alpha_5(1){\cdot}a_{11} + \alpha_5(2){\cdot}a_{21} + \alpha_5(3){\cdot}a_{31}\}{\cdot}b_1(\text{B})$

$= \{(2.916 \times 10^{-5} \times 0.3) + (2.69032 \times 10^{-5} \times 0.0)$

$+ (1.82112 \times 10^{-3} \times 0.0)\}0.2$

$= \{1.7496 \times 10^{-6} + 0.0 + 0.0\}$

$= 1.7496 \times 10^{-6}$

$\alpha_6(2) = \{\alpha_5(1){\cdot}a_{12} + \alpha_5(2){\cdot}a_{22} + \alpha_5(3){\cdot}a_{32}\}{\cdot}b_2(\text{B})$

$= \{(2.916 \times 10^{-5} \times 0.7) + (2.69032 \times 10^{-5} \times 0.4)$

$$+ (1.82112 \times 10^{-3} \times 0.0)\}0.5$$

$$= \{1.0206 \times 10^{-5} + 5.38064 \times 10^{-5} + 0.0\}$$

$$= 6.40124 \times 10^{-5}$$

$$\alpha_6(3) = \{\alpha_5(1) \cdot a_{13} + \alpha_5(2) \cdot a_{23} + \alpha_5(3) \cdot a_{33}\} \cdot b_3(B)$$

$$= \{(2.916 \times 10^{-5} \times 0.0) + (2.69032 \times 10^{-5} \times 0.6)$$

$$+ (1.82112 \times 10^{-3} \times 1.0)\}0.5$$

$$= \{0.0 + 8.07096 \times 10^{-5} + 9.1056 \times 10^{-4}\}$$

$$= 9.912696 \times 10^{-4}$$

From equation (7.9), the Baum–Welch probability P^{BW} of producing the counter colour sequence is

$$P^{BW} = \sum_{j=1}^{3} \alpha_6(j)$$

$$= 1.7496 \times 10^{-6} + 6.40124 \times 10^{-5} + 9.912696 \times 10^{-4}$$

$$= 1.0570316 \times 10^{-3}$$

In the Viterbi algorithm, the calculation of $\phi_{t+1}(j)$ in equation (7.13) is similar to the calculation of the forward probabilities above except that a maximisation rather than a summation over previous states is used. Referring to the calculations above, it is possible to extract the values of $\phi_t(i)$ and the backtracking pointer $\mu_t(i)$.

$$\phi_1(i) = \pi(i) \cdot b_i(O_1)$$

$$\phi_1(1) = 0.24$$
$$\phi_1(2) = 0.02$$
$$\phi_1(3) = 0.0$$

$$\phi_{t+1}(j) = \underset{i=1,2,\ldots,N}{\mathrm{Max}} \{\phi_t(i)a_{ij}\} \cdot b_j(O_{t+1}), \quad t = 1, 2, \ldots, T-1$$

and

$$\mu_{t+1}(j) = \underset{i=1,2,\ldots,N}{\mathrm{ArgMax}} \{\phi_t(i)a_{ij}\} \cdot b_j(O_{t+1}), \quad t = 1, 2, \ldots, T-1$$

$$\phi_2(1) = 0.036 \qquad \mu_2(1) = 1$$
$$\phi_2(2) = 0.0672 \qquad \mu_2(2) = 1$$
$$\phi_2(3) = 0.0012 \qquad \mu_2(3) = 2$$

$\phi_3(1) = 0.0054$ $\mu_3(1) = 1$
$\phi_3(2) = 0.011264$ $\mu_3(2) = 2$
$\phi_3(3) = 0.004224$ $\mu_3(3) = 2$

$\phi_4(1) = 0.000324$ $\mu_4(1) = 1$
$\phi_4(2) = 0.0042688$ $\mu_4(2) = 2$
$\phi_4(3) = 0.0064032$ $\mu_4(3) = 2$

$\phi_5(1) = 0.00002916$ $\mu_5(1) = 1$
$\phi_5(2) = 0.000246352$ $\mu_5(2) = 2$
$\phi_5(3) = 0.001478112$ $\mu_5(3) = 2$

$\phi_6(1) = 1.7496 \; 10^{-6}$ $\mu_6(1) = 1$
$\phi_6(2) = 5.38064 \; 10^{-5}$ $\mu_6(2) = 2$
$\phi_6(3) = 9.1056 \; 10^{-4}$ $\mu_6(3) = 3$

Therefore the Viterbi probability P^V of producing the colour sequence is

$$P^V = \underset{i = 1, 2, 3}{\text{Max}} \{\phi_6(i)\} = 9.1056 \times 10^{-4}$$

Thus the model is in state 3 when it produces the last observation. Backtracking from this state using the backtracking pointer shows that the state sequence is 1, 1, 2, 2, 2, 3.

7.3.2 Training hidden Markov models

The training of a HMM model involves assuming an initial estimate of the model, M, by assigning values to the elements of the π, A and B matrices and then by re-estimating the model on presenting it with known training sequences. For each training sequence O, the parameters of a new model M_{new} are re-estimated from those of the old model M_{old}, until M_{new} is a better model of the training sequence O than M_{old}, that is

$$Pr\{O|M_{new}\} \geq Pr\{O|M_{old}\} \tag{7.15}$$

At each iteration, M_{old} is replaced by M_{new} and another re-estimation takes place, until the above equation is satisfied. For proper training of each model, it is necessary to train the model with many tokens of the same word and perhaps even present the same data over and over again.

A detailed study of HMM training algorithms is beyond the scope of this text. However, a set of parameter re-estimation formulae for one particular algorithm, the Baum–Welch or forward–backward algorithm are quoted below, without any development or proof that they are guaranteed to improve the probability of the model producing the training sequence.

In the Baum–Welch algorithm, the transition matrix $\{a_{ij}\}$ is re-estimated using the formula

$$\{a_{ij}\}_{\text{new}} = \frac{\sum_{t=1}^{T-1} \alpha_t(i)\{a_{ij}\}_{\text{old}} b_j(O_{t+1})\beta_{t+1}(j)}{\sum_{t=1}^{T-1} \alpha_t(i)\beta_t(i)} \tag{7.16}$$

where T, $\alpha_t(i)$ and $\beta_t(O_{t+1})$ are as previously defined and refer to the training sequence. The quantity $\beta_t(i)$ defines a set of *backward probabilities* which are the joint probabilities of starting in state i at time t and then completing the observation sequence, starting with O_{t+1} and ending with O_T, that is

$$\beta_t(i) = Pr\{O_{t+1}, O_{t+2}, \ldots, O_T, \text{state } i @ t+1 \mid M\}$$

$$= \sum_{j=1}^{N} a_{ij}b_j(O_{t+1})\beta_{t+1}(j), \, t = T{-}1, T{-}2, \ldots, 1 \tag{7.17}$$

The state symbol matrix $\{b_{jk}\}$ is re-estimated using the formula

$$\{b_{jk}\}_{\text{new}} = \frac{\sum_{t @ O_t = P_k} \alpha_t(j)\beta_t(j)}{\sum_{t=1}^{T} \alpha_t(j)\beta_t(j)} \tag{7.18}$$

where $t @ O_t = P_k$ means sum over all values of t at which the observation O_t is equal to the codebook pattern P_k. Thus only those pattern probabilities which occur in the training sequence are re-estimated. Finally, the re-estimation formula for the initial state probability matrix is

$$\pi\{i\}_{\text{new}} = \frac{1}{P^{\text{BW}}} \alpha_1(i)\beta_1(i) \tag{7.19}$$

7.4 Speaker identification/verification

A problem closely related to automatic speech recognition is that of automatic speaker identification (ASI) and automatic speaker verification (ASV). ASI is the process of determining the identity of the input voice, whereas the task in ASV is to verify whether the spoken voice matches the identity of the speaker being claimed. ASI and ASV therefore involve recognition of the speaker's voice, rather than recognition of what was actually spoken. Therefore, these systems aim to exploit differences in voice quality and style of speaking rather than to attempt to normalise or eliminate them, as is the case in automatic speech recognition.

Speaker identification/verification systems operate in a very similar manner to the speech recognition systems described in the previous sections. Both types of system have a training or enrolment phase, where features relevant to speaker identity are extracted and stored. A set of reference patterns or templates for N known speakers is stored in the system and pattern matching techniques are used to compare the input voice template with the stored template. Speaker identification becomes more difficult as the size of the speaker population increases, since the input template must be compared with each of the N stored templates. In speaker verification, on the other hand, the input template is compared with one identified reference template. There is simply a single binary (yes/no) decision and the system performance is independent of the number of speakers.

The performance of both speaker identification and speaker verification systems is determined also by the type of input speech material. In fixed-text systems, the user recites pre-determined words or phrases, whereas in free-text systems, there are no restrictions on what is said and the input template has to be compared with stored templates for totally different utterances. In addition, fixed-text systems are primarily used in access control applications, where the user is co-operative and generally consistent from session to session, whereas free-text systems are normally used in forensic and surveillance applications, where the subject is non-co-operative and often unaware of the task. It might be expected therefore that fixed-text systems give a much higher level of performance than free-text systems.

The most critical aspect in the design of speaker identification/verification systems is the choices of features to be used in the template representation. Ideally, the features should be easy to measure, stable with time and relatively unaffected by the operating environments, but should not be copyable by impostors. Human recognition of speakers' voices is based on inherent features, mainly arising from vocal-tract size and shape, and also on learned features, such as dialect, speaking rate etc., which are connected chiefly with the dynamics of vocal-tract movement. Unfortunately, many of the learned features can be mimicked by impostors, so further care has to be taken. Since the parameters and features used in automatic speech recognition also contain information about the speaker, most of these already encountered in speech recognition can be used for speaker identification/verification. Linear prediction coefficients, their derivatives and transformations, formant frequencies, cepstral coefficients, spectral magnitudes, energy profiles etc. have all been used with some success. Studies have shown that an optimum feature set should ideally include formant frequencies and pitch. However, both of these can be difficult to extract accurately, particularly in unfavourable conditions. Pitch has the added problem of being easy to mimic, though the mean value of pitch computed over time has been used successfully. Some dynamic vocal-tract features which have been found useful for ASI and ASV are degree of co-articulation during the production of nasals, formant slope in diphthongs, voice onset time for voiced stops and speech-burst durations, where a 'burst' refers to a period when the energy in the signal exceeds a threshold value.

In most fixed-text systems, reference templates for each speaker are stored as a time-sequence of frames of the multi-dimensional (typically 8–14) feature vector. Some systems simply use one template per speaker averaged (clustered) over a number of repetitions of the word during training. Better performance can be obtained by storing templates of several utterances and/or several tokens of the same utterance. Time alignment and pattern matching can be carried out, using a dynamic time-warping (DTW) algorithm. Pattern matching may also be carried out, using the technique of hidden Markov modelling.

Another pattern-matching approach which has been found useful for both text-dependent and text-independent systems and, indeed, speech recognition is that of *codebook recognition*. This approach makes no attempt to time-align utterances. Instead, a separate vector codebook for each speaker/word combination is derived from one or more utterances of the word. For speaker recognition, the input word is vector-quantised against all the codebooks and, in ASI systems, the speaker corresponding to the codebook which gives the lowest distortion is selected. In ASV systems, the codebook distortion is compared against a threshold. Although timing information is lost, this technique is successful, even in free-text systems, because the codebook for each speaker is likely to contain large numbers of commonly occurring spectral patterns, which are distinctive to his/her voice.

Since the input and reference templates in free-text systems never correspond, the templates in these systems are often derived from parameters based on long-term statistics of the speech signal, rather than from a time-sequence of frames. This involves obtaining a single average template of pitch and spectral information, from all the available data for a given speaker. Unfortunately, the method is not suitable for real-time applications, as utterance lengths of the order of at least 30 seconds are required to gather the statistics.

Speaker verification has already been achieved on a commercial scale, but at the time of writing (1992), this is not the case for the more difficult problem of speaker identification. A number of fixed-text systems are available which can achieve the speaker rejection and impostor acceptance rates of less than 1 per cent, when used for access control to secure installations by user populations of up to 200 speakers. A typical enrolment time is 2–3 minutes and verification time is typically under 10 seconds.

One of the greatest application areas for speaker verification is over the telephone network for activities like tele-banking and remote access to computing facilities over dial-up telephone lines. Unfortunately, the performance of speaker verification systems over the telephone network is not as good, owing to the reduced signal bandwidth, noisy channel and also the distortion introduced by the various types of microphone used in telephone handsets. The best speaker rejection and impostor acceptance rates currently available are of the order of 5 per cent and 1 per cent respectively. Clearly, a lot of research needs to be carried out to determine the mechanisms of human speaker recognition and to relate these mechanisms to features which can be extracted from the speech signal.

7.5 Future trends

The foregoing sections have indicated the enormity of the problem of achieving human-like performance in automatic speech recognition. In spite of this, speech recognition has now (1992) reached a point where commercial systems have been developed and are being utilised in certain applications. These systems have restricted vocabularies (typically less than 1000 words) and generally use some form of finite-state grammar to limit the number of words that have to be matched at a given point in an utterance. The average number of words to be matched is referred to as the *perplexity* of the system and for current commercial systems, the perplexity is typically 50–60. Both speaker-dependent and speaker-independent, isolated word systems are available and some offer a connected-word capability, though the recognition performance in this mode is considerably reduced. A few large-vocabulary, isolated-word, speaker-independent systems have also been developed commercially. These have vocabularies of the order of 30 000 words and some are speaker-adaptive, in that, on encountering a new speaker, they initially use the stored, speaker-independent templates and dynamically adapt these during on-line speech recognition.

The earliest systems to appear on the market were based on dynamic time-warping (DTW), but more recently, systems based on hidden Markov modelling (HMM) have begun to appear. HMM is currently the predominant approach in speech recognition, because of its superior recognition performance and lower computational load for speech recognition (but not training). Claimed recognition accuracy for current commercial systems is typically of the order of 95 per cent, though this depends a great deal on the vocabulary of the applications, the operating environment and the experience of the user. Some systems are designed specifically to operate in noisy, stressful environments, such as the cockpits of fighter aircraft, and in such an environment can achieve very creditable recognition performances in excess of 90 per cent.

Virtually all of the systems available commercially are word-based, in that the vocabulary items are stored in the form of whole-word templates and are, at best, connected-word systems, rather than continuous speech systems. A number of laboratory continuous (sentence) recognition systems based on sub-word units (syllables, demi-syllables, phonemes, diphones, triphones) have been successfully developed. These systems are application-specific and operate with vocabularies of about 1000 words with perplexities ranging up to about 60.

At the time of writing (1992), probably the most successful laboratory-based continuous speech recognition system is the SPHINX system, developed at Carnegie–Mellon University in the United States [Lee, 1989]. This is a speaker-independent continuous speech recognition system with a vocabulary of 997 words. The system is based on obtaining trained hidden Markov models for 1100 generalised sub-word (triphone) units. (A triphone is a speech sound (phone) with both its right context and left context transitional properties included.) HMM–word-models are constructed by putting together appropriate triphone models, and sentences are constructed from the word models, in accordance with a finite state grammar of the application, which is a naval resource management task, in which information on position and status of various ships in the US Pacific fleet may be obtained from a database using spoken commands. Speech recognition is based on a Viterbi algorithm, which obtains the optimum path through the HMM–word network. The computational load in the recognition process is reduced by a 'pruning' technique, which involves traversing a number of paths in parallel. When the cumulative probability for a path falls below a set threshold, it is eliminated (beam search). Thus, only the best paths are traversed and the sentence corresponding to the highest probability is selected as the recognised sentence. The SPHINX system has a word-recognition accuracy of 95 per cent and a sentence recognition accuracy of 80 per cent.

7.5.1 Front-end processing

Research has shown that the front-end signal-processing stage is of crucial importance to the performance of a speech recognition system. The choice of parametric or feature extraction method affects both the recognition accuracy and the robustness of the system to noise. Different parameters have different statistical and separability properties, which are affected differently by the application vocabulary and the range of speaker accents which the system must accommodate. At present, there is no clear consensus on what are the optimum parameters to use, though many researchers favour a set of 8–12 cepstral coefficients, spaced on a non-uniform (mel) frequency scale, and consequently called *mel-frequency cepstral coefficients* (MFCCs). In addition, individual parameters within a particular type set have different perceptual significances. Obviously, perceptually more important parameters should be weighted more heavily than lesser important ones in the pattern-matching process. This involves weighting each element of the feature vector by the appropriate factor. An extension of this technique, which has also been found beneficial, is to obtain a linear transformation of the feature vector. The transformed feature vector is obtained by multiplying each input feature vector by a matrix with the elements of the matrix being chosen to maximise the difference between phonetically different features and at the same time minimising the effect of feature variation due to speaker differences and operating environment. A comprehensive programme of research is required to determine the optimum parameters to use and the optimum values of perceptual weighting and transformation coefficients.

Another approach, which is beginning to show promise in front-end processing in speech recognition, is to model the human auditory system. Humans exhibit a powerful ability to recognise speech even in very noisy environments. Research is being conducted to derive computational models of the periphery of the human auditory system. These models try to simulate, either directly or indirectly, the spectral analysis performed by the motion of the basilar membrane, and take into account such neural firing phenomena as adaptation, lateral suppression and masking. A number of studies have shown that a speech recognition system with a front-end auditory processor gives better performance than more conventional parametric techniques in high levels of ambient noise.

7.5.2 Hidden Markov models

It seems almost certain that, in the near future, hidden Markov modelling (HMM) will virtually replace dynamic time-warping (DTW) in speech recognition. DTW-based systems incur relatively little computational expense during training and substantial computational expense during recognition. By contrast, HMMs require computationally intensive training, but relatively simple recognition procedures. Given adequate training, the performance of HMM systems is generally better than that of DTW systems. The storage requirements of HMM systems is also substantially less than for DTW systems.

There is strong evidence to suggest that, in the future, the performance of HMM-based systems can be improved in a variety of ways. A mixture of continuous probability density functions (PDFs), each characterised by its mean and variance, can be used to replace the discrete output symbol PDF $\{b_{jk}\}$. These are known as *semi-continuous hidden Markov models* (SCHMMs). The advantage of SCHMMs is that the number of parameter values to be estimated from the training data is substantially reduced, which leads to better statistical models for the same amount of training data.

One problem with standard HMMs is that they cannot model word duration variations, which are important for distinguishing certain words. For example, the words 'bad' and 'bat' are distinguishable by their relative vowel durations. The incorporation of duration into HMMs to produce what are known as *hidden semi-Markov models* (HSMMs) gives slightly better performance.

Increased recognition performance in HMMs can also be obtained through the use of multiple codebooks. Instead of producing a standard output feature symbol at each time-frame, the model might output multiple symbols, including dynamic features. Research has already shown that the use of frame-to-frame differential features in conjunction with the normal static features can give improved performance. Since the HMM produces multiple symbols at each time-frame, the overall output symbol probability is computed by multiplying the individual symbol probabilities, assuming that all output PDFs are independent.

The HMM technique has already been extended successfully to model sub-word units. In particular, the use of triphone units to model both intra-word and inter-word co-articulation effects (SPHINX system) indicates that, by using more detailed sub-word models, which utilise existing phonological knowledge, it may be possible to build large-vocabulary continuous speech recognition systems.

The importance of adequate training for HMMs has already been mentioned. For optimum performance, the statistics of the training data must be representative of the speech which the system will have to cope with during recognition. Much effort therefore will have to be devoted to acquiring large training databases containing different speakers of different type, different accent etc. It is also possible to obtain better speech models by optimising the training algorithm. The forward–backward (Baum–Welch) algorithm adjusts the transition and symbol output probabilities until the likelihood of the model producing the training data is maximised. The problem with this type of maximum likelihood estimation (MLE) is that it will not produce good speech models if the HMMs themselves are not true models of the training data and HMMs are not true models of real speech. It has been shown that a corrective training algorithm, which is based on maximising the model's recognition performance on the training data, rather than on maximising the likelihood of it having generated the training data, gives increased performance. It may be possible to develop other improved learning algorithms.

7.5.3 Neural networks

Neural networks are pattern-matching devices with processing architectures, which are based on the neural structure of the human brain. A neural network consists of simple interconnected processing units (neurons). The strengths of the interconnections between units are variable and are known as weights. Many architectures or configurations are possible, though a popular structure is that shown in figure 7.14, which is known as a *multi-layer perceptron* (MLP). The processing units are arranged in layers consisting of an input layer, a number of hidden layers and an output layer. Weighted interconnections connect each unit in a given layer to every other unit in an adjacent layer. The network is said to be feedforward, in that there are no interconnections between units within a layer and no connections from outer layers back towards the input.

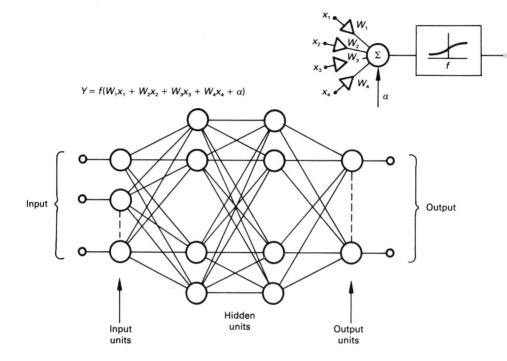

Figure 7.14   Multi-layer perceptron

The output of each processing unit, Y_j, is some non-linear function, f, of the weighted sum of the outputs from the previous layer, that is

$$Y_j = f\left\{\sum_{i=0}^{N-1} W_{ji}X_i + \alpha_j\right\}, \qquad j = 0, 1, 2, \ldots, N-1 \qquad (7.20)$$

where α_j is a bias value added to the sum of the weighted inputs and f represents some non-linear function, such as the tangent function. Thus, by adjusting the weights W_{ji}, the MLP may be used to represent complex non-linear mappings between a pattern vector presented to the input units and classification patterns appearing on the output units. In pattern-matching applications, the network is trained by presenting a pattern vector at the input layer and by computing the outputs. The output is then compared with some desired output, that is a set of output unit values, which will identify the input pattern. This is normally carried out on the basis of a particular set of output units being above a certain value. The error between the actual output and the desired output is computed and back propagated through the network to each unit. The input weights of each unit are then adjusted to minimise this error. This process is repeated until the actual output matches the desired output to within some pre-defined error limit. Many pairs of training input/output patterns are presented to the network and the above process is repeated for each pair. Training a neural network therefore requires large amounts of training data and very long training times, which can sometimes be several hours. Pattern recognition involves presenting the unknown pattern to the input nodes of the trained network and computing the values of the output nodes which identify the pattern.

Neural networks of various topologies have already been applied with some success to isolated-word recognition and sub-word unit recognition. The general performance that has been obtained so far is not quite as good as that of dynamic time-warping or hidden Markov modelling. However, this research is still in its infancy and better performance ought to be possible in the future.

7.5.4 Speech understanding

The speech recognition systems described so far are acoustic pattern-matching devices, in which speech properties are captured in a statistical way by training the system on representative data. Considering the human ability to recognise speech, it is unlikely that recognition systems based exclusively on this approach can ever hope to emulate human performance. Although the exact mechanism of human speech perception is not yet fully understood, it is clear that we use many sources of knowledge in decoding an utterance. Two of these main sources may be broadly classified as linguistic knowledge and semantic knowledge. Linguistic knowledge is concerned with the syntax (grammar) and phonology (sounds) of the language, and semantics refers to the meaning conveyed by the words.

In some speech recognition systems, the output is simply a transcription of the input utterance but an additional goal in many applications is to elicit some useful response from the system in the form of a reply (written or spoken) or perhaps even in the form of a physical action (such as a voice-controlled robot). In fact not all of the words need to be transcribed accurately, as long as the meaning is understood. If the response is correct, the system may be said to have 'understood' the input utterance. However, a machine capable of a real understanding of continuous human speech would require an enormous amount of real-world (semantic), linguistic and other knowledge, working in conjunction with a mechanism for decoding the acoustic patterns.

A number of simple speech understanding systems have been built, based on tightly constrained application domains, such as rail or airline timetable enquiry systems. Such systems typically incorporate several interacting knowledge sources, including acoustic, phonological, phonetic, prosodic, lexical, syntactic and semantic knowledge sources. These attempt to exploit the existing body of knowledge about speech, in particular knowledge about the relationship between acoustic features and higher-level linguistic representations, that is phonemes, syllables etc. This complex relationship is not very well understood. The human brain has an amazing ability to normalise extremely variable acoustic features and identify them from a small set of linguistic units. It is also not yet clear how best to represent or use in a computational framework the limited speech knowledge that is available. In the systems that have been developed to date, this knowledge has been represented in the form of a set of rules for each knowledge source. It might be possible in the future to embody it in a neural network, though very large networks and long training times will undoubtedly be required.

Of particular importance in speech understanding systems is the representation of semantic knowledge. Semantic knowledge is extremely difficult to formalise and represent. In tightly constrained applications, it is possible to represent it in a rudimentary fashion by having a model or internal representation of the application in which world knowledge is represented as states. The semantics processor has a mechanism for defining these states and updating them.

Since the real-world knowledge of current speech understanding systems is very limited, particular care has to be taken in the design of the dialogue management. The interaction must appear easy and natural to the user, yet he or she must not be given the impression that the system knowledge and language capability is greater than is actually the case, otherwise the complexity of the questions and replies will cause the system to misunderstand and perhaps fail in the task. The function of the dialogue management therefore is to constrain the semantic and linguistic content of the user's input speech. This will be an important aspect in the design of speech understanding systems in the immediate future. It is clear, however, that by human comparison, these systems will be of limited intelligence. Emulation of human intelligence by a machine may one day be possible but will probably take several generations to achieve.

Two suitable sources for further reading in Automatic Speech Recognition are the books by Ainsworth (1989) and Holmes (1987).

Problem

7.1. For comparing two speech patterns $P_1(n)$ and $P_2(m)$, a particular speaker verification system based on dynamic time-warping (DTW) uses the Itakura local path constraint illustrated in figure 7.4(b) and pattern distances are calculated using the 'city-block' distance metric.

Write down the corresponding DTW algorithm and use it to compute the difference between the one-dimensional patterns $P_1(n) = \{5, 2, 2, 6, 3, 5\}$ and $P_2(m) = \{4, 3, 3, 2, 8, 5\}$. Determine also the time-alignment paths.

References

Ainsworth, W.A. (1974). 'Performance of a speech synthesis system', *Int. J. Man–Machine Studies*, **6**, pp. 493–511.

Ainsworth, W.A. (1989). *Speech Recognition by Machine*, Peter Peregrinus, Hitchin.

Allen, T., Hunnicut, M.S. and Klatt, D. (1987). *From Text to Speech: The MI Talk System*, Cambridge University Press, Cambridge.

Atal, B.S. and Hanauer, S.L. (1971). 'Speech analysis and synthesis by linear prediction of the acoustic wave', *J. Acoustical Society of America*, **50**, pp. 637–655.

Bridle, J.S., Brown, M.D. and Chamberlain, R.M. (1983). 'Continuous connected-word recognition using whole word templates', *Proc. IERE*, **53**, pp. 167–175.

Cooley, J.W. and Tukey, J.W. (1965). 'An algorithm for the machine calculation of complex Fourier series', *Mathematics of Computation*, **19(90)**, The American Mathematical Society, Providence, Rhode Island.

Flanagan, J.L. (1972). *Speech Analysis, Synthesis and Perception*, Springer-Verlag, New York.

Gold, B. and Rabiner, L.R. (1969). 'Parallel processing techniques for estimating pitch periods of speech in the time-domain', *J. Acoust. Soc. Amer.*, **46**, pp. 442–448.

Harris, F.J. (1978). 'On the use of windows for harmonic analysis with the discrete Fourier transform', *Proc. Inst. Electrical and Electronic Engineers*, **66(1)**, January.

Holmes, J.N. (1980). 'The JSRU Channel Vocoder', *Proc. Institute of Electrical Engineers*, **127(F1)**, February, pp. 53–60.

Holmes, J.N. (1985). 'A parallel-formant synthesiser for machine voice output', in Fallside, F. and Woods, W.A. (eds), *Computer Speech Processing*, Prentice-Hall, Englewood Cliffs, New Jersey, pp. 163–187.

Holmes, J.N. (1987). *Speech Synthesis and Recognition*, Van Nostrand, Wokingham.

Ishizaka, K. and Flanagan, J.L. (1972). 'Synthesis of voiced sounds from a two-mass model of the vocal cords', *Bell. Syst. Tech. J.*, **51(6)**, pp. 1233–1268.

Kingsbury, N.G. and Amos, W.A. (1980). 'A robust Channel Vocoder for adverse environments', *IEEE 1980 Int. Conf. Acoustics, Speech and Signal Proc.*, pp. 19–22.

Klatt, D.H. (1980). 'Software for a cascade/parallel formant synthesiser', *J. Acoust. Soc. Amer.*, **67(3)**, March, pp. 971–995.

Lee, K.F. (1989). *Automatic Speech Recognition: The Development of the SPHINX System*, Kluwer Academic Publishers, Boston, Massachusetts.

Linggard, R. (1985). *Electronic Synthesis of Speech*, Cambridge University Press, Cambridge.

Lynn, P.A. and Fuerst, W. (1989). *Introductory Digital Signal Processing with Computer Applications*, Wiley, New York.

Markel, J.D. (1972). 'The SIFT algorithm for fundamental frequency estimation', *IEEE Trans. Audio Electroacoust.*, **AU-20**, pp. 367–377.

Markel, J.D. and Gray, A.H. (1976). *Linear Prediction of Speech*, Springer-Verlag, New York.

Mermelstein, P. (1973). 'Articulatory model for the study of speech production', *J. Acoust. Soc. Amer.*, **53(4)**, pp. 1070–1082.

Myers, C.S. and Rabiner, L.R. (1981). 'A level-building dynamic time-warping algorithm for connected word recognition', *IEEE Trans. Acoustics, Speech and Signal Proc.*, **29**, pp. 284–297.

Papamichalis, P. (1987). *Practical Approaches to Speech Coding*, Prentice-Hall, Englewood Cliffs, New Jersey.

Sakoe, H. (1979). 'Two-level DP matching – a dynamic programming-based pattern matching algorithm for connected-word recognition', *IEEE Trans. Acoustics, Speech and Signal Proc.*, **27**, pp. 588–595.

Tobias, J.V. (1970). *Foundations of Modern Auditory Theory*, Vols 1 and 2, Academic Press, London and New York.

Witten, I.H. (1982). *Principles of Computer Speech*, Academic Press, London and New York.

Zelinski, R. and Noll, P. (1977). 'Adaptive transform coding of speech signals', *IEEE Trans. Acoustics, Speech and Signal Proc.*, **ASSP-25(4)**, August, pp. 299–309.

Index

acoustic-tube model 111
adaptive
  delta modulation (ADM) 32, 33, 123, 135
  differential pulse code modulation (ADPCM) 30, 31, 123, 125
  pulse code modulation (APCM) 28, 123, 135
  transform coder 126
affricate 9
aliasing 18
allophone 7, 103, 105
allophonic variation 10, 86, 103, 105
analysis-by-synthesis 134
anti-aliasing filter 21
articulatory
  gesture 7–9, 86
  model 111
aspirated sounds 4
auditory
  canal 13
  nerve 4
  system 13–16
autocorrelation
  function 58–9, 82, 84
  method 61–3
  values 61, 62
average magnitude difference function (AMDF) 83, 84

basilar membrane 14
Baum–Welch
  algorithm 156
  probability 156, 157
beam search 150, 167
bilinear transformation 40–3
bipass filtering 75
biquadratic filter 94
Bridle algorithm 150–1
Butterworth filter 22

centre-clipping 82

cepstral
  analysis 53–8, 130
  smoothing 56, 75
  truncation 53
  vocoder 130
cepstrum 54, 56
Channel Vocoder 38, 127–9
characteristic impedance 116
Chebychev filter 22, 84
city-block distance metric 144
clustering 146
co-articulation 9–10, 86, 103, 105, 107, 108, 111, 139
cochlea 14
codebook 73, 136, 155
  recognition 165
codec 26
code-excited linear predictive (CELP)
  coding 136
companding 25
  characteristics
    A-law 26–7
    μ-law 26–7
composite response 38
constant-Q 15
continuously variable slope delta modulation (CVSD) 33
covariance method 63
critical band 15–16

damping 11
decision rule 147
delta modulation 31–4
demi-syllable 107
diaphragm 4
differential pulse code modulation (DPCM) 29–30
diphone 107
diphthong 8
directed graph 151
discrete cosine transform (DCT) 125
discrete Fourier transform (DFT) 44–50

dynamic programming   142, 143
dynamic time-warping (DTW)   140–6

eardrum   13
elliptic filter   22
endpoint detection   72, 139
energy function   70–1
Euclidean distance metric   73

fast Fourier transform (FFT)   50–3
feature extraction   70–87
FFT butterfly   51
filter
   bipass filtering   75
   biquadratic   94
   Butterworth   22
   Chebychev   22, 84
   elliptic   22
   filterbank   37–44
   finite impulse response (FIR)   43
   infinite impulse response (IIR)   42
   inverse   67, 84, 134
   lattice   101, 132
   median of N 85
formant   5
   synthesiser   92–9
   tracking   74–8, 130
fricative   4, 9
front-end processing   167–8

glide   7
glottal impedance   116
glottis   3
granular noise   32

hair cells   14
Hamming window   47
Hanning window   84
hard-limiter   31
heat-conduction losses   114
hidden Markov model (HMM)
   152–63
higher-formant correction   96

impulse invariant transformation   96,
   120
instantaneous adaptation   28
Integrated Services Digital Network
   (ISDN)   17
International Phonetic Alphabet
   (IPA)   7
intonation   10, 106, 139
inverse filter(ing)   67, 84, 134
isochronous foot theory   106

Itakura
   distance metric   74
   local path constraint   143, 145, 148

K-nearest-neighbour (KNN) rule   147

larynx   3
lateral suppression   16
lattice filter   101, 132
LBG algorithm   74
letter-to-sound rules   110
level-building algorithm   148–50
linear filtering   54
linear prediction   29, 59–67, 100–1,
   130–6
   code-excited (CELP)   136
   multi-pulse   134
   residual-excited (RELP)   135–6
linear predictive analysis (LPA)
   59–67
   autocorrelation method   61–3
   covariance method   63
linear predictive coding (LPC)   29,
   130–6
linear predictive synthesis   100–1, 132
linguistic knowledge   171
liquid   8
log-area ratio (LAR)   132, 133
losses   11
   heat-conduction   114
   viscous   114
   wall-vibration   114
LPC-10 vocoder   132–4
lungs   4

magnitude function   70
Marconi Channel Vocoder   129
Markov chain   152, 154
masking   15–16
maximum likelihood
   classification   154
meatus   13
mel-frequency cepstral coefficients
   (MFCCs)   16
mid-sogittal plane   112
modes of excitation   4
   random-noise   4
   transient   4
morph   110
multi-layer perceptron   169, 170
multi-pass filtering   75

nasal (sound)   4, 9

nasal tract   3
nearest-neighbour (NN) rule   147
nerve-endings   14
neural firings   14
neural network   169–71
neutral vowel   5
Nyquist frequency   21
Nyquist's sampling theorem   18, 123

observation   152
observation sequence   154
one-stage algorithm   150–1
oral tract   3
ossicles   14
oval window   14
oversampling   22

parallel formant synthesiser   97–9
pattern
    classification   147
    matching   140
perceptron   169, 170
perceptual weighting   134
perplexity   166
phase-shift keying (PSK)   27, 28
phone   107
    deletion   139
    substitution   139
phoneme   7–9, 86–7, 138
phonetic
    analysis   85–7
    lattice   87
pinna   13
pitch   4
    extraction   78–85
        autocorrelation methods   81–4
        Gold–Rabiner   79–81
        SIFT algorithm   84–5
    synchronous analysis   67, 68
plosive (sounds)   5, 9
pole frequency   76, 78
pole–zero model   67
pre-emphasis   36–7
pre-sampling filter   21–2
pre-warping   40, 41, 42
principle of optimality   143
probability density function   24, 168
pronunciation rules   110
prosodic pattern   103, 106, 107
prosody   10, 108
public services telephone network
    (PSTN)   17

pulse code modulation (PCM)   17
    adaptive differential (ADPCM)   30,
        31, 123, 125
    differential PCM (DPCM)   29–30

quantisation   17, 22–8
    adaptive   28–9
    adaptive differential   30–1
    differential   29–30
    logarithmic   25–8
    uniform   23–5
    vector   72–4
quantiser step-size   23
quefrency   54

radiation
    impedance   6, 114
    model   115
rectangular window   46
reflection coefficient   101, 116, 132
relaxation mode   4
residual-excited linear predictive
    (RELP) coding   135–6
resonant cavity   4
Reynold's number   119
rhythm   10, 106, 139
rib-cage   4

sample delay operator   36
sampling   18–21
sampling theorem   18, 123
segmentation and labelling   86
semantic knowledge   171
semivowel   7
serial formant synthesiser   96–7
short-time
    analysis   35
    energy function   70–1
    magnitude function   70
signal-to-noise ratio (SNR)   24–5
slope overload   32
soft-windowing   46, 82
source–filter model   5–7
speaker
    adaptive   140
    identification/verification   163–5
spectral leakage   46
spectrogram   11, 12
speech coding
    adaptive transform coder   126
    CELP coder   136
    cepstral vocoder   130

Channel Vocoder 127–9
formant vocoder 129–30
LPC-10 vocoder 132–4
multi-pulse coder 134
RELP coder 135–6
subband coding 123–5
transform coding 125–7
vector-quantiser coder 136
speech recognition
  connected-word 139, 147–52
  continuous 139
  dynamic time-warping
    (DTW) 140–6
  hidden Markov model
    (HMM) 152–63
  isolated word 139, 140
  speaker-dependent 139
  speaker-independent 139, 140, 146,
    147
speech synthesis
  articulatory 88, 111–20
  by rule 103
  concatenation 107–8
  copy 101–2
  phoneme 102–7
  text-to-speech 108–11
speech synthesiser
  formant 92–9, 129, 130
  JSRU 98
  Klatt 99
  linear predictive 100–1
speech understanding 171–2
SPHINX system 166, 167
stop-consonant 9
stress 10, 108, 139
sub-word unit 167, 169, 171
syllabic adaptation 28
syllable 107
syntax tree 151

terminal-analogue synthesiser 88
tertiary clipping 82
Toeplitz matrix 62
trachea 3

transform
  discrete cosine 125
  discrete Fourier (DFT) 44–50
  fast Fourier 50–3
  inverse discrete Fourier 45
  inverse Z 41
  Z 36
transient excitation 5
travelling wave 116
triphone 167
turbulent air-flow 119–20
twiddle factor 51
two-level algorithm 148
two-mass model 117
tympanic membrane 13

unitary matrix 126
unvoiced sounds 4

vector quantisation 72–4, 136, 152,
  155
velum 3
viscous losses 114
Viterbi algorithm 157
vocal cord model 111
vocal cords 3
vocoder
  cepstral 130
  Channel 38, 39
  LPC-10 132–4
Voder 89
voiced sounds 4
vowel 7

wall-vibration losses 114
window
  Hamming 47
  Hanning 84
  rectangular 46
windowing 46
  soft 46
windpipe 3

zero-crossing rate 71–2